Praise for *Son of Satan*

Dr. Scudder has written a gripping presentation of the final end-times world ruler known as the Antichrist. In convincing fashion, he shows how the Antichrist will rise to power through seduction, persuasion and clever propaganda. And he explains in detail what the Antichrist will declare on those Christians who are on earth during the Tribulation. In the closing pages, we catch a glimpse of his utter defeat at the hands of the Lord Jesus Christ. This book will strengthen your faith and cause you to say, "Even so, come Lord Jesus!" Buy two copies—one to read and one to give to a friend.

Dr. Ray Pritchard, Senior Pastor
Calvary Memorial Church
Author of *An Anchor for the Soul, Man of Honor*, and *And When You Pray*

How prophecy will be fulfilled is the subject Dr. Scudder deals with in his new book, *Son of Satan, The Coming Economic Prosperity.* The author insists that Bible prophecy is true, accurate, reliable, and shows that prophecy speaks of sin, salvation, judgment, and eternity. Many leading national and international prophecy scholars endorse this well-documented, Bible-based book. In a unique way, the author highlights the success of the deception of Satan and his Antichrist, wrapped in a package of peace and prosperity for the last days. This book is a must for all believers.

Arno Froese
Director, Midnight Call Ministries
Author of *Prophecy in the Law*, *The Coming Digital God*, and *How Democrac*

D0956186

With a pen of warm and fresh compassion, Dr. Scudder has marshaled the power of the Word of God and insight gained from decades of faithful ministry in writing this powerful book. Reading our daily newspapers mandates that we adopt a literal interpretation of biblical prophecy, and Dr. Scudder shows us why. In the midst of end-time chaos portrayed in these pages, echoes of a diabolical plan of evil contrivance fill the chambers of human government. Yet, the plan and purpose of a loving and sovereign God reverberate with an overpowering fulfillment of Bible prophecy. God has never lost control and Jesus will take His place with the government of the world resting on His Shoulder. You should read this book to see why Jesus alone is the earth's rightful king!

Carl E. Baugh, Ph.D.
Founder and Director, Creation Evidence Museum

Dr. Scudder's chilling insights and powerful storytelling have given me a whole new perspective on the Bible's end-time prophecies. After studying *Son of Satan,* I'm more determined than ever to see to it that no one I know will be left un-raptured to be tortured in the grasp of the Antichrist's reign of terror.

Julie-Allyson Ieron
Author of *Praying Like Jesus*
and *Staying True in a World of Lies.*

I have just finished reading for the second time Dr. Scudder's book, *Son of Satan*, which relates in a highly readable and enjoyable fashion the events that will occur during the final history of the earth, as described in the book of Revelation. This book was inspired by Dr. Scudder's interest in prophecy and sharpened by his reading of 100 books, which describe these last days. We both believe that the book of Revelation is a literal account of what will really happen to the earth. I highly recommend this book.

Duane T. Gish, Ph.D.
Senior Vice President, Institute for Creation Research
Author of *The Fossils Still Say No!* and
Creation Scientists Answer Their Critics

For the believer, this book is a spiritual stimulus, reminding us that we are on the winning team.

R. Larry Moyer
President and CEO, EvanTell Inc.
Adjunct Professor in Evangelism,
Dallas Theological Seminary
Adjunct Professor in Evangelism, Word of Life

I whole-heartedly endorse this book. It is exciting to study about the next event on God's calendar, the Rapture.

Art Rorheim
Founder and President Emeritus
Awana Clubs International

SON OF SATAN

OTHER BOOKS BY JAMES A. SCUDDER

Beyond Failure
Your Secret to Spiritual Success
The End of Time
More Than a Miracle

SON OF SATAN

THE COMING
ECONOMIC PROSPERITY

BY JAMES A. SCUDDER

Victory In Grace Publishing
Lake Zurich, Illinois

Son of Satan
The Coming Economic Prosperity

Published by: Victory In Grace Publishing
                 60 Quentin Road
                 Lake Zurich, IL 60047
                 www.victoryingrace.org
                 1-800-784-7223

All Scripture quotations are taken from the Holy Bible: King James Version.

Editorial Services by:
Julie-Allyson Ieron, Joy Media

Cover Design by: Jay Bensen

ISBN: 0-9719262-1-2
Library of Congress Control Number: 2004100947

First printing 2004

Printed in the United States of America

Contents

Acknowledgements

A special thank you to the team at Victory In Grace Ministries for their dedication to this project. Also, I wish to thank Julie Scudder Dearyan, Daniel Darling, Rev. Mike Floyd, Barb Vanden Bosch, and Kari Kumura for contributing to the editing of this book. Julie-Allyson Ieron and Joy Scarlatta Ieron provided their excellent editorial services as well. Jay Bensen designed the cover while Daniel Reehoff laid out the inside. We are truly fellow laborers in Christ and through His love can accomplish great things for Him. It is my prayer that this book brings encouragement and blessing to every reader.

Chapter 1

The Advent

New York City
Daniel 11:21

THE WORDS PREPARED HIM FOR LATER. "Yes. I'm ready," he said to the white-shirted waiter. Ready now. His thirty-year obscure sojourn had ended. Soon he would look out upon the world and invite them to listen to the person who cared, the only human being in the universe who had the answers. They wanted to hear him. He imagined standing before them as they stared at their television sets in their living rooms around the world. Timed perfectly, flashing on prime time news, he would stand on the Temple Mount, poised, confident. Later they would film him at a local wedding, the bride and groom standing beneath the traditional cloth. It was the perfect kick-off. People would put away their sorrow for that time for they would want the bride and groom to be joyful. And so, during that happy, swirling occasion, his ministry would begin and the world would wonder and believe.

The ones who would have hindered me have been taken away, he thought. He remembered wandering as a boy along the river bank near his home. He knew even then. He was called to something higher. A tiny rock had felt smooth in his hand. He had flung it across the water picturing himself as the stone skipping across the water to the applause of millions. It would be a miracle. He would impress them with his power. And he would do what others had done, only he would do it better. He would feed the hungry around the world for a time, shelter the homeless, comfort the distressed with real deeds, not useless platitudes, for he would know how to assuage the strongest fears. He would bring hope to a world that had lost its hope.

They would have to follow him. Especially now that they hurt. Thousands were going insane having lost spouses, children, babies, and lovers. The newscasters didn't know what to say; even those who wrote the headlines in newspapers around the world couldn't capture the horror.

He chuckled softly as he stood and walked toward the café door. He strolled down the street toward a high-rise. Some thought he came from Rome, others from Paris, still others from New York. He had lived in every city but now he was going to the home no one knew about. He touched the button on the elevator and stepped inside thinking about the power he craved. He was at the top of his own game, a self-made man. He thought about all those who had gone before. Martyrs to the cause. Jannes and Jambres. Herod. Elymas the Sorcerer. And of course, the ultimate, Judas, indwelled by the most high himself. He would outshine them all.

He tapped his pager signaling his arrival. Even as he looked out from the roof, he could tell the city was reeling from shock. It was the middle of the afternoon, but most businesses were closed. Groups of people stood in the street weeping as they held onto each other. His face grew hard for the briefest second as he wondered why people missed the Christians at all. His own grandmother had been one. He was glad she was gone.

The helicopter was waiting. And so was someone else. A tall woman with her head bowed.

"I'm Olivia Andrews." She said, "I wonder if I could take a moment of your time."

Andrews' face was filled with suffering.

"Of course. What can I do for you?" His voice was carefully modulated. He had learned from the best how to make his voice ache with emotion and sound strong and powerful—almost within the same moment.

"My daughter. She was only 13."

His black-suited guard was waiting to swing open the helicopter door but he knew better than to rush the moment.

"Only 13," he echoed.

"She's gone. One of the missing. I don't know what to do. When I went to the police, they told me that they couldn't help because they were dealing with thousands of such cases." Her voice broke. "I know you to be a man who knows a lot of powerful people." He looked down and noticed her hand rested on a headline about him in the paper. Yes, his PR people were doing okay thanks to the millions of dollars he fed them.

She continued. "My uncle is the police force head. He told me that he had heard you were going to leave from here for Jerusalem. He thought maybe you could give me some hope."

He forced himself not to appear irritated. She couldn't know how crucial the timing was at this moment. Maybe he could use this conversation in the speech he was going to make later. It would give all the hurting people something to latch onto.

He took a slim card from his coat. "Here." He looked deep into her eyes. He knew his own power. She stared back at him, and then he saw a hopeful glimmer appear. Good. She would help him in his cause. Tell her friends and family that he was the man for this hour.

"Use the number on this card at any pay phone to get an instant update on your daughter's status. I will put her case on prime alert. I know how important this is to you."

She gripped the card with both hands. "How can I ever thank you?" But he was already being whisked into the helicopter.

He sat staring at her upturned face as they took off. A strange power filled his limbs. His breath felt charged with excitement. Only a few more minutes and he would arrive at his Learjet where he would be transported to Israel.

The world weeps now, but they will embrace me once they see all that I offer, he thought, *Your plans are going perfectly, Satan. I am but a tool in your hands.*

* *

HIS BRILLIANCE WILL ASTOUND THE WORLD, BUT IT WILL BE HIS COMPASSION THAT WILL STEAL THEIR HEARTS. He will possess all the traits touted by the psychological community as the epitome of success, self-love, self-acceptance, and self-esteem, but no one will think he is prideful. He will appear in control of his own destiny, yet he will seem approachable. His honest demeanor will attract the hard-working element, while his diabolical side will bring those tinged with evil. His godlike powers will bring the religious to their knees, and they will accept him wholeheartedly—calling on the world to do the same. He will talk favorably of religion, sharing his personal meditative rituals with every religious group. He will share traits of them all and will know to highlight those qualities without offending those who don't believe in God.

His warm laugh and sense of humor will have television and radio networks begging to interview him. His knowledge of global affairs will dumbfound the powerful, and his simple kindness to world leaders will bring about astounding reconciliation. Countries whose rivalries with other ethnic groups go back for centuries will say, "This man's love is bringing us together." Each nation will love him, for he will be a man of them all, yet the Bible tells us that Israel will feel a special kinship. A kinship so close that they will look at one another and say, "Rejoice, our Messiah has come." They will sacrifice once again in the ancient way; and as they do so, thanks to his uniting powers even the Muslims, Hindus, and Catholics will look on these actions benevolently. He will have flattered them all, promising that he is for them, too.

His plan of allegiance will seem like the height of concern. "Take my special mark," he will say. "You will finally be safe. You will be able to track your loved ones, so they will never be lost like that crazy right-wing fringe was only a few years ago." He will explain that the mark will cut crime rates to almost nothing, because there will be no need for cash. He will explain that men and women's power will be in their hands or foreheads. It will all be so easy. Go to the grocery store without your purse. Attend that favorite sporting event without your wallet. You won't have to worry about someone stealing your money any more or someone assuming your identity with a stolen credit card. Humankind will finally have the utopian godless society longed for since the fall.

People will take the mark even as they begin to see that not everything this man does is peaceful. As he assures them that no one needs to fear, nations fight like never before. He wins the kingdom by peace, but he sustains it by war.

He is the Son of Satan. The embodiment of Satan's plan that began the moment he fell from Heaven. This is the Antichrist. Not just "against" Christ, he is the ultimate humanistic christ, the kind of man people have always wanted. He will be the bionic man, the six-million dollar man, and the best clone from the best people who have ever lived, all wrapped up in one smooth, svelte package.

His imitation of Christ's earthly pilgrimage will be peerless, adding further clout to his profile. He will claim a virgin birth, have his own three-and-a-half-year ministry, perform signs and wonders, have his own unholy trinity, and his own death and resurrection. This imitation will fool both the religious and nonreligious, for mankind is looking for such a man—one who will bring all the divisions and strife together in one big, happy whole.

NEARING THE PRECIPICE

Watch out for this man! He could be alive today, though he won't reveal himself until after the Rapture of the Church. Will people know this man is the Antichrist, the Son of Satan? This is the chilling truth. The world won't know, at least at first. The Bible says that if it were possible the very elect, or the church itself, would be deceived by the Son of

Satan. People won't look at him and shout, "That man is evil! Don't go near him! Don't do what he says! Don't listen to him!" Instead, the world will applaud him, admire him, and adore him. I venture to say that if you came face to face with the Antichrist today, you would love him immediately. You probably would think, *That is the nicest man I have ever met.* For unlike other evil men who hide, this man will be so good at evil that he will look perfectly good. He will stand on the busiest street corners in the world shaking hands and winning hearts. He will be an Angel of Light in whom no one detects a shadow, at least for a while. For a short time this man will be to the world what Christ is to believers. A savior. A deliverer. A mighty prince. A wonderful counselor.

For all his apparent kindness, in his heart he is a deceiver, just as his father the Devil is a fraud. One day, the hammer will fall and human-kind will know the horrifying truth. They will have been led as sheep to the slaughter when he deceives them into taking his mark. Now that same mark, far from promising security and ease, dooms them to death and destruction.

CAN I ESCAPE?

Although the Philippine army had virtually encircled them, Abu Sayyaf rebels and their three hostages (one Filipino nurse, Deborah Yap, and two New Tribes missionaries, Martin and Gracia Burnham) slipped past the army to another island in May 2002. The three hostages had been held for almost a year, having been taken from a seafront hotel by this rebel group. To their horror, some hostages had been beheaded while others were randomly released. The Burnham family negotiated a large sum of money for their release, but they just ended up losing their money. Scared that the rebels would stage another escape, the government mounted a raid. In the process, the hijackers used the Burnhams and Yap as human shields. Martin and the nurse were fatally shot during the rescue. Gracia received a wound in the leg from her captors but was rescued.[1] It was an amazing rescue for

Gracia, but you can only imagine her sorrow at seeing her husband and friend shot to death before her eyes.

I'm sure Martin and the others wanted desperately to escape their horrific captors, yet for most there was no escape. When the Son of Satan arrives to set up his kingdom, there will be no escape for the world. Your chance to escape is now. Will you take it?

He Hasn't Come Yet, So Why Should I Worry?

There are those who say that since the world has waited for these events for over 2,000 years, why should anyone worry about it ever happening? If you look at many churches today, there is apathy toward coming prophetic events. Many denominations even teach that the Rapture won't occur. Some groups teach that if we all work together to reform the world, when it reaches a certain point Christ will come back to rule and reign.

Dr. M.R. De Haan, the founder of Radio Bible Class, came from this background. After a few years, he began to study the Bible and learned about the imminent return of Christ. This doctrine changed his outlook. He spent many years preaching on the subject and writing books about prophecy. He never quite believed that he would leave the world by the undertaker. He often said that if he did die, he hoped to be buried near someone who held theological views differing with his concerning the imminent, Pre-Tribulation Rapture.

"Then I can say as we are caught up to be with the Lord, 'I told you so!'" he (De Haan) would quip with his half smile. "But then, I probably wouldn't really do that, for God says we'll all be changed in the twinkling of an eye."[2]

De Haan's former beliefs aren't unusual today even among some Bible believing and teaching churches. Many people don't understand that the false teachings concerning the end times that abound today are only further proof that the Bible is accurate. Scripture teaches that in the last days there would be indifference toward the Rapture. Far from keeping this event from happening, these false teachers are right in line with what the Bible predicts. Not only is it exciting that the Rapture will occur at any moment (possibly before you finish this sentence), but it is more exciting to understand that God predicted the current indifference. Matthew 24:37-39 explains the climate before the Rapture, "But as the days of Noah were, so shall also the coming of the Son of man be. For as in the days that were before the flood, they were eating and drinking, marrying and giving in marriage, until the day that Noah entered into the ark, and knew not until the flood came and took them all away, so shall also the coming of the Son of man be." It says people will be eating, drinking, marrying. In other words, just as people turned off Noah's warnings about the upcoming flood and instead chose to eat, drink, and marry as if nothing were going to happen, so people will be in the coming generation before the next great event on the prophetic timetable.

THE THEFT NO ONE NOTICED

Not long ago, thieves stole valuable wrought iron gates from St. Barnabas Church in London. A few weeks before, a set of antique wooden gates were taken from St. Joseph's church in the same town. Both thefts were carried out without anyone noticing anything unusual. The police think the burglary happened in daylight, because the passersby thought the gates were being removed for repair and didn't even notice what the thieves looked like.[3] When I read this article, I couldn't help but compare these thefts to how Jesus describes the Rapture of the Church. Just as casual observers didn't notice the thefts even though they happened in broad daylight, so most church members won't notice that there are many signs of the Great Tribulation happening right before their eyes.

When I was a new believer and I learned about the coming events on God's calendar, I got so excited I could hardly stand it. I remember hearing phrases like, "I'm not looking for the undertaker, I'm looking for the uppertaker!"

and "It's going to be a Rapture, not a rupture, Church are you ready?" I remember how thrilled I was to understand that there would be one group of people who would not die. I found out that I could possibly be a part of that group.

A few years ago I was having lunch with a couple who had been saved for many years. We started to speak about current events and how they fit into prophecy when the wife turned to me. "I don't know what all this fuss is about," she said. "We've been hearing about Christ's coming for a long time now. It's all hype as far as I'm concerned."

I wanted to shout, "This isn't hype! It's truth! Jesus Christ will return. You might wish to continue to live your life the way you've planned it. You may think you have days or even years to complete your goals and worldly ambitions, but don't you understand: Jesus could take us to Heaven at any moment?"

The Apostle Peter prophesied this attitude when he wrote, "Knowing this first, that there shall come in the last days scoffers, walking after their own lusts, And saying, Where is the promise of his coming? for since the fathers fell asleep, all things continue as they were from the beginning of the creation" (2 Peter 3:3-4).

One prophecy scholar says Christ "warned that He would come when the Church would be characterized by sleepy complacency and when many would even be entertaining wishful thoughts of a delay of His return. It would be a time when He was least expected and even His own were in danger of being caught by surprise."[4]

How you feel about the Lord's coming doesn't affect whether this event will occur. Even the Apostle Paul called his time frame the "last days," and they were the last days. This is one of the last periods of history. When the Rapture happens, only 1007 years remain for this earth.

A lady visited a specialist one day. While she was filling out the paperwork, her little daughter happened to look over at what she was doing. She noticed that there were five boxes. The first box said, "0-20 years of age," the next said,

"21-29 years of age," the next said, "30-39 years of age," the next, "40-49 years of age." The last box said, "50 and beyond." The little girl noticed that her mother checked the box for 40-49 years of age. "Mother," she said, "do you realize that you are in the next to last box of life?"

Dear friend, do you understand that you are in the next to last box of God's timetable? We are in a time like no other, the end of the last days. This exciting thought should purify your walk with Christ. As you grasp the thought of the Rapture, it should bring you an urgency to live in what could be for you personally, the next to last box of life.

READY FOR DEPLOYMENT

Bible teacher and author, Charles U. Wagner says this, "When Scripture tells him (the believer) to 'look for that blessed hope' he can do so with a confidence that allows this hope to impact his life spiritually. His pace in evangelism and missions is quickened knowing that he is commanded to serve the Lord while waiting for the Son from Heaven (see 1 Thess. 1:10). He does so with a vision that is not vague, a hope that is not in vain, and an assurance that when Christ comes there will be ultimate and final victory."[5]

One pastor who has served in the military compared the Rapture to what the military does before deployment. Imagine that the sergeant in charge of the duty roster calls you at home and tells you to get to the base ASAP. He tells you to bring all your gear minus your field jacket and sleeping bag, and says to kiss your wife and kids goodbye for a while. You have two hours to get your affairs in order. The clock starts ticking. You can't find your jungle boots. The Sergeant had hinted that you are going somewhere warm because he said not to bring your field jacket. The pressure is mounting because if you are not there in less than 120 minutes—ready to go to the staging area—you will be considered AWOL. You start searching for your bug spray. You ask your wife to help you find it, and you search the house. Finally, you find the missing items, and the wife and kids take you to the battalion. You wonder for a brief moment if you really are going to be deployed. You are. You ask the first sergeant, "Where are we going?" He says, "You'll know when you get there. It's not for you to know right now."[6]

The readiness you would feel standing there with all your gear, equipped to go at any moment is precisely how believers should feel about the Rapture. We need to get our combat boots, our bug spray, and our affections loosed from earthly things. We need to care for the lost, trying to bring them to Christ. Then we are equipped as Christ tells us to be. We are set for deployment to that higher plane!

THREE HELPS FOR YOUR DEPLOYMENT

Perhaps you picked up this book out of curiosity. You don't know much about the end times, but you want to learn more. I commend you for that. God promises a blessing to those who study prophecy. Maybe you are a student of the Word, and you want to learn more about this diabolical ruler to come, the Son of Satan. Again, this book will give you much information that will help you in your spiritual walk. Whatever the case, a prophecy study should do three things: calm our fears, generate enthusiasm about the accuracy of the Word, and motivate believers toward holy living.

I'M AFRAID! WHAT SHOULD I DO?

Just a quick look at the headlines of newspapers around the world should jolt you into understanding that the time of "Jacob's Trouble" as the Tribulation is called, is near. Here are some recent ones, from the *New York Times*, "Car Bomb Kills a British Banker in Saudi Arabia"; from *The Jerusalem Post*, "Four Family Members Slain in Itamar Infiltration"; from BBC News, "Car Bombs Rock Southern Spain," "Bangladesh President Resigns." And these are just a few examples.

The truth is, we are living in a scary world. Crime rates are soaring like never before; murder in the womb is considered the obvious choice; guns are brought to school and used on teachers and fellow students; earthquakes are increasing in frequency and duration; walls of wildfire devastate homes and miles of forest; deadly floods wipe out thousands; and the list goes on. How do we deal with such bad news? How do we cope in a world that seems to be spiraling out of control?

The answer might seem simple at first, but delve a little deeper and you will begin to see that the study of prophecy will change your life. If you are a believer, the thought of the Rapture should bring peace to your greatest fears. Paul calls the Rapture the "blessed hope" in Titus 2:13, and there is a reason he does so. Understand that you are a part of the Church, the Bride of Christ. You will be caught up with Christ in the clouds before the Son of Satan is revealed. The early church exulted in this knowledge, rejoicing in the hope of the Rapture.

First Thessalonians 2:19 explains, "For what is our hope, or joy, or crown of rejoicing? Are not even ye in the presence of our Lord Jesus Christ at his coming?"

James tells us more when he says, "Be patient therefore, brethren, unto the coming of the Lord. Behold, the husbandman waiteth for the precious fruit of the earth, and hath long patience for it, until he receive the early and latter rain. Be ye also patient; stablish your hearts: for the coming of the Lord draweth nigh" (James 5:7-8). The word *patience* in this verse means to forbear, to wait. And I think I could add here the thought, to be calm. God holds the future in His palm, and in the midst of the chaos, He desires that you rejoice in His glorious hope.

Todd was a bright young college student who had recently trusted Christ as His Savior. He told me that before he was saved, he worried constantly about the future. He was concerned about someday bringing children into a world that seemed more corrupt than it had been when he was young. Then he learned about the future events on God's calendar. Now he sees the signs around him as exciting, realizing that he is living in the latter end of the last days. Knowing about Jesus' soon return has calmed his fears. And so it should calm yours. The old saying, "Don't look to the future, look to the One Who holds the future," couldn't be more true than during the current unrest and evil.

Will you take a minute right now to thank the Lord for giving you prophecy? Will you ask Him to help you take what you learn and use it to help calm your fears about the future? He will help you for that is one reason He had the Apostles write about your blessed hope.

PROVING THE WORD, ESPECIALLY NOW

Sarin Ahmad, a 20-year-old computer student was ready to execute a deadly plan. She was to become a martyr while blowing other people to pieces in Israeli streets. Her terrorist handlers told her to "be brave" and "to pray" while they showed her the 22-lb. bomb she was supposed to strap to herself. After she and a 16-year-old boy were delivered to the site, both had second thoughts. Ahmad shared with *La Stampa*, an Italian newspaper, that she suddenly thought of her intended victims as humans, too. The two potential bombers phoned their contact in the terrorist group and said they didn't want to go through with the plan. The contact rejected their decision. Ahmad said, "They said we must die." The 16-year-old tragically carried out the orders. He and three others were killed. Ahmad dropped the bomb in an abandoned car and fled.[7]

While it is refreshing and unusual to hear that Ahmad chose not to use that bomb, the fact that Israel daily experiences suicide attacks and other atrocities is proof of how true the Word of God is. Daily, world news centers on Israel. We are seeing more and more people turning against this tiny nation. Saddam Hussein said just before the war in Iraq, "I proudly and respectfully salute the heroes of martyrdom operations (suicide bombings) who give their lives for Palestine and the Arab nation." He also paid tribute to the "Palestinian women who joyfully bid their children farewell" before staging suicide attacks.[8]

The fact that Israelis have gathered once again in their land is one of the biggest miracles of our time. There were books written prior to 1947 that stated in effect, "There is no way there will be a return of Israel to her land." And yet, we know much to the world's amazement, that in 1948 the Jewish nation was established. One author says, "Nearly 1900 years after the last destruction of the nation of Israel and the scattering of her people all over the earth, the nation of Israel is in place once again in the land that God gave to her nearly 4000 years ago. It is a restoration unique in human history, in fulfillment of numerous and specific prophecies, and it bears the unmistakable imprint of the hand of God."[9]

Zechariah 12:2-3 predicts what is happening today, "Behold, I will make Jerusalem a cup of trembling unto all the people round about, when they shall be in the siege both against Judah and against Jerusalem. And in that day will I make Jerusalem a burdensome stone for all people: all that burden themselves with it shall be cut in pieces, though all the people of the earth be gathered together against it."

Jeremiah 30:10-11 states, "Therefore fear thou not, O my servant Jacob, saith the Lord; neither be dismayed, O Israel: for, lo, I will save thee from afar, and thy seed from the land of their captivity; and Jacob shall return, and shall be in rest, and be quiet, and none shall make him afraid. For I am with thee, saith the Lord, to save thee: though I make a full end of all nations whither I have scattered thee, yet will I not make a full end of thee: but I will correct thee in measure, and will not leave thee altogether unpunished."

Jeremiah 31:35-36 explains that only if the sun and the moon cease, will God forget Israel. "Thus saith the Lord, which giveth the sun for a light by day, and the ordinances of the moon and of the stars for a light by night, which divideth the sea when the waves thereof roar; The Lord of hosts is his name: If those ordinances depart from before me, saith the Lord, then the seed of Israel also shall cease from being a nation before me for ever."

Not long ago, The European Executive Union published a survey of its attitudes on Iraq and world peace. They found that 59 percent saw Israel as a threat, putting it above Iran, North Korea, and the United States. The poll also found that 68 percent of EU citizens believed the U.S.-led invasion of Iraq was not justified.[10]

Do you see how Jerusalem is a "burdensome stone" to the world today? When the majority of the European Union nations see Israel as a threat greater than Iran or North Korea, you know the end is near.

We should study prophecy because it comprises so much Scripture. Look at the following statistics:

- Approximately one-fourth of the Bible was prophetic when it was written.
- Of the 333 prophecies concerning Christ, only 109 were fulfilled at His First Coming, leaving 224 yet to be fulfilled at His Second Coming.
- There are a total of 1,527 Old Testament passages referring to the Second Coming.
- In the New Testament, 330 verses refer directly to the Second Coming of Christ.
- The Lord Himself refers to His return 21 times in Scripture.[11]

These facts alone tell us how vital a thorough study of prophecy is to the believer.

Your Motivation

As I mentioned before, when I learned about the Rapture, I couldn't believe how much the Lord cared for His Bride, the Church. But it also did something else for me. The more I studied how imminent this event was, so grew my desire to live a holy life. The Apostle Paul writes in 2 Timothy 4:8, "Henceforth there is laid up for me a crown of righteousness, which the Lord, the righteous judge, shall give me at that day: and not to me only, but unto all them also that love his appearing." When you consider how close His appearing is, it will motivate you to live a holy life.

A pastor named Vernon Grounds writes, "A friend told me something that happened while he was in seminary. Since the school didn't have a gymnasium, he and his friends played basketball in a nearby public school. Nearby, an elderly janitor waited patiently until they finished playing. Invariably he sat there reading his Bible. One day my friend asked him what he was reading. The man answered, 'The book of Revelation.' Surprised, my friend asked if he understood it. 'Oh, yes,' the man assured him. 'I understand it!' 'What does it mean?' he asked. Quietly the janitor answered, 'It means that Jesus is gonna win.'"[12]

Dear friend, you know the ending. You know Jesus is going to win. You know every single thing He predicted is going to happen. And you can let that hope purify your soul and inspire you to live a life honoring and pleasing to the Lord Jesus.

Do you need to stop right now and recommit your life to the Lord? Maybe you've skipped your devotional time lately, and you want to get back on track. Perhaps you haven't attended church for a long time, and you wish to restore fellowship with other believers. It could be that you are in a backslidden condition, and you want to cry out to the Lord asking Him to help you serve Him. Maybe you desire to commit yourself again to your wonderful Christ, this One who has saved you from death and Hell and promises to either take you up in the Rapture or bring you to Heaven when you die. Whatever your situation right now, why don't you take a moment to pray this prayer?

Lord, I want this study of the Antichrist to be real to me. I desire for it to inspire me to witness to others. I ask that the thought of Your soon return will help me live a pure life.

READY TO BE REVEALED

During a sweltering summer, my air-conditioning unit failed. We had moved into a condominium and had purchased some insurance that went along with it. The insurance was supposed to cover any repairs needed on our appliances. Since nothing had gone wrong in the last year, when the renewal notice came for the insurance, I thought about not signing it. After all, most of the appliances were virtually new and probably wouldn't need repair. After some deliberation, however, I decided to sign up for the insurance.

The next day my air-conditioning failed. I called the repairman for our group of homes, and he said that he would be coming out in a day or two. A day or two passed, and he didn't show up. I called again, and he came. He looked at the unit and informed me that the insurance wouldn't cover the repairs needed on the unit and that this was going to cost me $4,000. I couldn't believe it. I thought this was why people pay for insurance in the first place! I was informed by another repair place that I could get the parts I needed for about $1,000. That seemed like a better deal, so I made an appointment with him to check out my air conditioner. I had to schedule it just before church on a Wednesday night. I thought I could just swing it if he came and left promptly. He never showed up, and I barely made it to church. By this time summer was in full swing and anyone who knows anything about me knows I like to keep the temperature in the home at about 60 degrees.

I was sweltering. Sunday came and went without any repairman showing up. This was getting irritating. Finally, he came out saying he was sorry, he just had a backlog of work. Thankfully, he fixed my air conditioner, but I learned something from that encounter. The constant heat kept me aware of my need for air conditioning. Apply this thought to how we think about the Rapture. We see some of the signs of things to come; the more we learn about what is going to happen, the more ready we will be.

One day soon, a man will stand in the Holy of Holies in the Jewish Temple, and he will desecrate it. He will declare himself to be God and the Jewish people will know that they have accepted a satanic imposter and brought him into leadership. They will understand how blinded they have been and they will flee, hiding their face from this evil man, but many won't be able to escape.

THE MAN OF SIN

In this book you will learn about the Son of Satan. You will see Satan's plot since the beginning of time to sabotage God's plans. And you will start to put the pieces of the puzzle together, understanding that the Man of Sin is the epitome of everything Satan wants in a man. You will learn more about his political genius, his commercial master plan, his evil designs for Israel, his death and resurrection, and his final ruin and destruction.

But you don't have to be caught up in that ruinous scene. You can disengage yourself from it by being sure you will be with Christ before the Son of Satan begins his grisly reign.

Who would ever dream of amputating his own leg? Nobody—unless that person had lost his mind or was faced with the grim choice of losing either his leg or his life. That was Bill Jeracki's terrible predicament, according to *The Denver Post*, when he was out fishing alone in the foothills of the Rocky Mountains. He was trapped when a boulder fell on his leg, and he was unable to free himself. Knowing that as night came on he might die of exposure, Bill did what he knew he had to do. Relying on his skill as an assistant to a doctor at a Denver hospital, he took a nylon rope out of his tackle box, tied it tightly above his knee, and cut off his leg with his knife. He then dragged himself to his car and drove ten miles to the nearest town. He not only survived the trauma, but with an artificial limb he is out fishing again.[13]

What a decision—your leg or your life! But what if the stakes were even higher? What if you had to choose between trying to do good deeds to go to Heaven and accepting salvation? The choice might seem obvious, but many people are depending on good works or their religion to get to Heaven instead of relying on the finished work of the Lord Jesus Christ. God sacrificed His only Son to pay the price for our sins. Choosing to believe in the shed blood of Christ will guarantee that you will be taken up to Heaven before the Great Tribulation or when you die, you will go to Heaven. Won't you decide right now to trust Christ as your Savior? His death, burial, and resurrection paid the price for your sins. He is begging you to trust Him. Why don't you take a moment and do that right now? Then you can warn others of this great imposter, the Son of Satan, ready to be revealed.

FREE
full-color Prophecy Chart

✔ Yes, Dr. Scudder! Please send me a FREE full-color Prophecy Chart.

My Name

Address

City   State   Zip

Email   Phone

What I've enjoyed about *Son of Satan, The Coming Economic Prosperity:*

Dr. James A. Scudder • Victory In Grace Ministries
60 Quentin Road • Lake Zurich • IL • 60047
1-800-78GRACE • www.victoryingrace.org

Dr. James A. Scudder

Dr. Scudder, please send me a
free full-color Prophecy Chart

BUSINESS REPLY MAIL
FIRST CLASS MAIL   PERMIT NO.68   LAKE ZURICH, IL   60047

POSTAGE WILL BE PAID BY ADDRESSEE

Dr. James A. Scudder
Victory In Grace Ministries
60 Quentin Road
Lake Zurich, IL 60047-9966

Chapter 2

The Sign

Eternity Past
Isaiah 14:12-16

WINGS STRETCHED AROUND THE THRONE AND THE CREATURES SHONE AS THEY WORSHIPPED. Some cried out for joy, others clasped their hands, hundreds knelt, their hands stretched forward.

"You are worthy, O Lord!" The words echoed into eternity.

He thought how his heart had echoed those words so many times. He looked at the flowing river, deep, clear, reflecting the rubies, emeralds, garnets, and diamonds in the sky. He almost couldn't glance on His face; the glory was pure, true, overwhelming. He sensed the kindness, the mercy of God. That was one of the reasons he was the Guardian, the Keeper of the Glory.

A shadow crossed his face.

He bowed. "I must go."

Their eyes caught for a moment, but he broke the gaze first. For the first time since Creation, He couldn't look on His face. For reasons he didn't want to think about, the moment was pure pain.

"Leave, then."

The music resumed, a symphony of sound, each Creature performing with several instruments. Gabriel held a golden clarion in one hand, cymbals rested on his wings. The seraphim held one instrument for each of their heads, the notes blending, and bouncing, but the glorious praise didn't thrill him today. He used to lead the praise. His thoughts went to another part of Heaven. *God knows.* He didn't know where the thought came from. He adjusted his robe, heavy with jewels.

God knows why.

He brought his hand crashing through the clouds. He shook his head feeling moisture in his eyes but he forced back the tears. It didn't matter if God knew. It couldn't matter. God was the reason he had to do this. It was all God's fault.

He bowed his head and the atmosphere rushed past him.

God whispered to him, then. This way of communication used to delight his soul. "You have set yourself above me, O Lucifer, your pride has blinded you to what you had. Go."

He had been waiting for this moment, but he was surprised it had come so soon. He had been banished. He lifted his head outstretching his hands and legs toward the Heavens. Dazzling lightning flashed around him, deep rolls of thunder thudded at his feet. Meteors and comets halted in their hurtling flight. He shook his fist toward the throne. "I will exalt myself above You." As he said the words, thousands of angels plunged with him, their brilliant glow causing the space around them to fill with strange light.

There was no second chance. They would help him. He would save them for himself. They would bow; give him deserved obeisance. And they would destroy the Throne. He halted suddenly pulling himself before them all.

"I will ascend above the Most High. I am the Most High," he shouted. Instantaneous applause filled his heart.

The Most High. His new title. He was the Creator now.

He didn't want to notice that the universe was chilly, not warm and glowing like the throne. He knew the other beings were trying not to discern this.

"Come," he told them. "There is much to be done."

And they went out, not knowing from whence they came.

* *

FROM HIS FALL, SATAN HAS TRIED TO BECOME LIKE THE MOST HIGH. His desire to get back at God started the moment he fell from Heaven. Satan was, at one time, the highest angel. The great prophets, Ezekiel and Isaiah describe his past. He is called the "son of the morning," and his beautiful clothing is described in great detail. They picture an angel shrouded in God's glory and show his prideful heart.

- I will ascend into heaven.
- I will exalt my throne above the stars of God.
- I will sit also upon the mount of the congregation, in the sides of the north.
- I will ascend above the heights of the clouds.
- [Then the final atrocity] I will be like the Most High.

Though he had everything, though he was perfect in beauty, he chose to leave. The battle began at that moment. The created being combats the Creator. The created decides he is the Creator—possibly birthing the theory of evolution at that moment. With the power given to him to praise God, he wages war on the Almighty and His saints. We know the outcome. We, who read and understand God's Word, know that one day, Satan will be bound and thrown into Hell.

But make no mistake, the battle is real. It is still being fought. Right here. Right now. It is everywhere around us. It explains much of the wickedness of our age, of any age. Satan still wants to ascend above God. His ego is so great that he believes his own lies. He thinks he can destroy God.

One day, he will usher in his son, the epitome of all he stands for. For a while, it will look like Satan has finally succeeded, that he has converted the world to total, all-out adoration of himself.

For a time.

What happens before that time? We know Satan can even now enter into the outer courts of Heaven to accuse believers before the Throne, but it is the Church who ascends into the very presence of God at the time of the Rapture. I believe this Rapture, the next event on God's calendar, is just around the corner. We could be the generation that does not need an undertaker but rather an uppertaker.

THE SIGNS

Understand that the Rapture could have happened at any point since Christ ascended to Heaven. New Testament authors write longingly of His return. Paul says in 1 Corinthians 1:7, "So that ye come behind in no gift; waiting for the coming of our Lord Jesus Christ."

He says again in 1 Thessalonians 5:23, "And the very God of peace sanctify you wholly; and I pray God your whole spirit and soul and body be preserved blameless unto the coming of our Lord Jesus Christ."

Peter rebukes those who doubted Christ's return in 2 Peter 3:4, "And saying, Where is the promise of his coming? For since the fathers fell asleep, all things continue as they were from the beginning of the creation."

John writes in 1 John 2:28, "And now, little children, abide in him; that, when he shall appear, we may have confidence, and not be ashamed before him at his coming."

Authors of the famous *Left Behind* series, Tim LaHaye and Jerry Jenkins write,

> Ever since Jesus Christ warned His followers that He would leave them to go to His Father's house in heaven and promised that He would "come again and receive (them) to (Himself)," Christians have been asking the $64,000 question: "When will you return, and what will be the sign of your coming?" The fact that Jesus did not rebuke the disciples for asking those two questions indicates that He approves of our watching for the signs of His return. Daniel, the great Hebrew prophet, asked similar questions about end-time events in the twelfth chapter of his book.

A study of prophetic literature from the first century right up to our own day will show that Bible-believing Christians have always been interested in "when?" and the "signs." Admittedly, some commentators have come up with bizarre theories and conclusions that were proven wrong by the passage of time. Some have set ill-advised dates. In other cases, such as the Millerites in 1844, individuals have brought great embarrassment to the church. Most, however, have been humble teachers of the Word, who watched for sign-like events in their day in a vain hope that theirs would be the generation to see Christ return.

That hasn't been all bad. While some people became discouraged and quit studying prophecy because Christ had not yet returned in their lifetime, others were driven to restudy the Scriptures and became more conscious that Christ could return in their generation. This, in turn made them more conscious of holy living in their holy age, more evangelistic and more missionary-minded.[1]

And while it is true that Christ's return could have happened in any generation, even the most "non-tech" person can't miss that technology has advanced to a point that the Tribulation period events such as a worldwide monetary system and people tracking, could reasonably happen in the near future. At no other point in history could this be said with such confidence.

Prophecy expert, Dave Hunt, makes the following point. "Fanaticism and date setting are folly. It would seem to be at least equal folly, however, to ignore Christ's warnings about being caught by surprise. We are responsible, as every generation before us has been, to know the signs of His coming and to determine whether they are applicable to our day ... ours is the first generation to whom special signs Christ foretold could possible apply."[2]

Matthew 24:33 states, "So likewise ye, when ye shall see

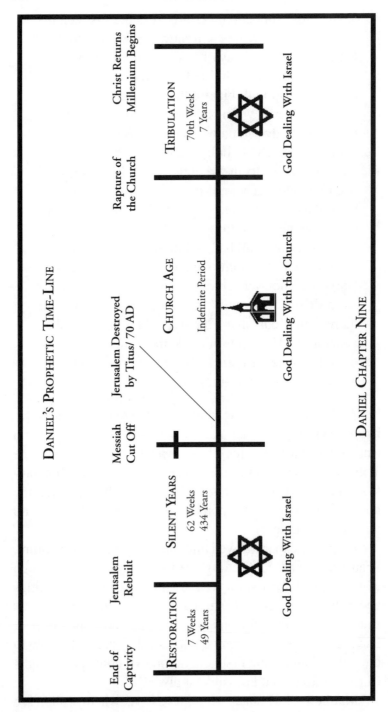

Daniel's Prophetic Time-Line

End of Captivity

Jerusalem Rebuilt

Messiah Cut Off

Jerusalem Destroyed by Titus/ 70 AD

Rapture of the Church

Christ Returns Millenium Begins

RESTORATION
7 Weeks
49 Years

SILENT YEARS
62 Weeks
434 Years

CHURCH AGE
Indefinite Period

TRIBULATION
70th Week
7 Years

God Dealing With Israel

God Dealing With the Church

God Dealing With Israel

DANIEL CHAPTER NINE

all these things, know that it is near, even at the doors." What are these signs that we would see? What are the events that would tell of the season of Tribulation period?

Remember this. While there are many signs for what is known as the Second Coming of Christ, there are no signs for the Rapture. Jesus described the Rapture as coming like a "thief in the night." He even went so far to say that only His Father in Heaven knew the exact moment. But we know that the Rapture is the event that begins the Tribulation period at the end of which is the Second Coming. The diagram on page 38 lays out God's plan as explained in Daniel 9.

Remember this. The Second Coming concludes the Tribulation period. During this time, God deals primarily with Israel just as He did before the death of Christ. This is one of the strongest arguments for the Pre-Tribulation, Pre-Millennial position. But the season for the Tribulation period with such events as a world-wide religion and monetary system can be felt even now.

Prophecy scholar Thomas Ice explains, "God's purpose for the tribulation (i.e., the seven-year, seventieth week of Daniel) revolves around His plan for Israel and does not include an earthly presence for the church. Why? Because God's plan for Israel is unfinished at this point in history. When the role of the church is completed, she will be taken as a completed body to heaven in an instant—at the Rapture. This will clear the way for a restoration and resumption of progress toward the completion of our Sovereign Lord's plans for His elect nation—Israel."[3]

While the Church has experienced and will experience tribulation and trouble during this present time, she is never mentioned in relation to "The Time of Jacob's Trouble" or the "Great Tribulation." Notice that even the name "The Time of Jacob's Trouble" mentions one of Israel's patriarchs. The emphasis of the Great Tribulation is Jewish. Here are just a few of the Scriptures that support this:

• Jeremiah 30:7 states, "Alas! for that day is great, so that none is like it: it is even the time of Jacob's trouble; but he shall be saved out of it."

- Daniel 12:1 explains, "And at that time shall Michael stand up, the great prince which standeth for the children of thy people: and there shall be a time of trouble, such as never was since there was a nation even to that same time: and at that time thy people shall be delivered, every one that shall be found written in the book."

- During the Olivet Discourse, Christ warned, "But pray ye that your flight be not in the winter, neither on the sabbath day: For then shall be great tribulation, such as was not since the beginning of the world to this time, no, nor ever shall be. And except those days should be shortened, there should no flesh be saved: but for the elect's sake those days shall be shortened. Then if any man shall say unto you, Lo, here is Christ, or there; believe it not. For there shall arise false Christs, and false prophets, and shall shew great signs and wonders; insomuch that, if it were possible, they shall deceive the very elect. Behold, I have told you before. Wherefore if they shall say unto you, Behold, he is in the desert; go not forth: behold, he is in the secret chambers; believe it not" (Mat. 24:20-26).

Notice the reference to Daniel's prophecy of the temple and the flight on the Sabbath. There are many more references contained in the earlier part of that passage to the twelve tribes of Israel, signs, the son of "Moses," and the "covenant with the Beast."

There are also many Old Testament prophecies yet to be fulfilled concerning Israel and her eventual salvation that will take place at the Second Coming and during the Millennium. If we take a position that is unfortunately becoming more common to the Church and say that the Church is Israel, then these prophecies will never be fulfilled. That statement in itself is against God's nature. The best way to interpret the Bible is from a literal standpoint where we interpret Israel as Israel and the Church as the Church. Therefore, when the Church is never mentioned in relation to the Tribulation period, what should we believe? That the Church is absent. Raptured.

THE CHURCH ABSENCE IN OLD TESTAMENT PROPHECIES

Not one Old Testament passage on the Great Tribulation mentions the Church. Yet here is one of the passages that clearly mentions Israel.

Jeremiah 30:4-11 says,

> And these are the words that the Lord spake concerning Israel and concerning Judah. For thus saith the Lord; We have heard a voice of trembling, of fear, and not of peace. Ask ye now, and see whether a man doth travail with child? wherefore do I see every man with his hands on his loins, as a woman in travail, and all faces are turned into paleness? Alas! for that day is great, so that none is like it: it is even the time of Jacob's trouble; but he shall be saved out of it. For it shall come to pass in that day, saith the Lord of hosts, that I will break his yoke from off thy neck, and will burst thy bonds, and strangers shall no more serve themselves of him: But they shall serve the Lord their God, and David their king, whom I will raise up unto them. Therefore fear thou not, O my servant Jacob, saith the Lord; neither be dismayed, O Israel: for, lo, I will save thee from afar, and thy seed from the land of their captivity; and Jacob shall return, and shall be in rest, and be quiet, and none shall make him afraid. For I am with thee, saith the Lord, to save thee: though I make a full end of all nations whither I have scattered thee, yet will I not make a full end of thee: but I will correct thee in measure, and will not leave thee altogether unpunished.

The New Testament does not speak of the Church in relation to the Tribulation either. In Matthew 13:39-43, Christ states, "The enemy that sowed them is the devil; the harvest is the end of the world; and the reapers are the angels. As therefore the tares are gathered and burned in the fire; so shall it be in the end of this world. The Son of man shall send forth his angels, and they shall gather out of his kingdom all things that offend, and them which do iniquity; And shall cast them into a furnace of fire: there shall be wailing and gnashing of teeth. Then shall the righteous shine forth as the sun in the kingdom of their Father. Who hath ears to hear, let him hear."

After Revelation chapter four, the Church is not mentioned at all. Why would this book mention so much about the Church in the first three chapters and then never mention her again? There is no question about it, the Rapture has occurred and now God is dealing primarily with His people, the Jews. So, now that we have established that the Church has to be gone for the Tribulation to begin, here are some of the reasons I believe that the season for this time is here.

Seventy Sevens

Daniel recorded one of the most comprehensive prophecies concerning what is called the "seventy sevens." Daniel was informed concerning how Israel related chronologically to the end of the times. He was told that there would be seventy sevens or seventy "weeks" that would occur from the time the city was rebuilt until the return of Christ.

In Scripture, a week is often referred to as a seven-year period. Jacob worked for Laban two "weeks" so Rachel would become his bride, but really he worked fourteen years. The Hebrew word *shabua* translated by our English word week literally means "seven." Therefore seventy weeks is seventy sevens. The context of the following passage determines that "sevens" is being used as a unit of time and refers to years. Sir Robert Anderson, an astute student of prophecy, worked out the dating of Daniel chapter nine in meticulous detail. His calculations can be found in his book, *The Coming Prince*. Anderson determined that the timing in Daniel works out perfectly from the rebuilding of Jerusalem until the week Christ rode on a donkey into Jerusalem. Take a moment now to read through this important passage.

Daniel 9:24-27 explains,

> Seventy weeks are determined upon thy people and upon thy holy city, to finish the transgression, and to make an end of sins, and to make reconciliation for iniquity, and to bring in everlasting righteousness, and to seal up the vision and prophecy, and to anoint the most Holy. Know therefore and understand, that from the going forth of the commandment to restore and to build Jerusalem unto the Messiah the Prince shall be seven weeks, and threescore and two weeks: the street shall be built again, and the wall, even in troublous times. And after threescore and two weeks shall Messiah be cut off, but not for himself: and the people of the prince that shall come shall destroy the city and the sanctuary; and the end thereof shall be with a flood, and unto the end of the war desolations are determined. And he shall confirm the covenant with many for one week: and in the midst of the week he shall cause the sacrifice and the oblation to cease, and for the overspreading of abominations he shall make it desolate, even until the consummation, and that determined shall be poured upon the desolate.

John Walvoord states,

> The accomplishment defined as "the finished transgression" most probably refers to Israel's tendency to apostasy, which must be brought to a close as Israel is brought to restoration and spiritual revival at the time of the Second Coming. Practically all pre-millennial expositors agree that the terminus

of this prophecy is before the future millennial kingdom. The ultimate restoration of Israel awaits their regathering at the time of the Second Coming. Obviously, the Old Testament sacrifices could not bring Israel to this important milestone, and it required the death of Christ on the cross establishing many details of the New Covenant for Israel.[4]

The beginning of the 490 years happened when Nehemiah rebuilt the wall and the city at 445-444 B.C. and this works out precisely to the fulfillment of the prophecy and also coincides with the actual rebuilding of the city. Four hundred and eighty three years after the city was rebuilt culminates in the year A.D. 33 where recent scholarship has placed the death of Christ.

At that point, there is a parenthetical period known now as the Church. This was a mystery not known before it was revealed fully to the Apostle Paul in Ephesians 3:3-6, "How that by revelation he made known unto me the mystery; (as I wrote afore in few words, Whereby, when ye read, ye may understand my knowledge in the mystery of Christ). Which in other ages was not made known unto the sons of men, as it is now revealed unto his holy apostles and prophets by the Spirit; That the Gentiles should be fellowheirs, and of the same body, and partakers of his promise in Christ by the gospel."

How do we know that this is a parenthetical time period? Because Jesus Christ's death and resurrection made possible this new union of Jews, Gentiles, bond, and free into His body. The Holy Spirit now indwelled believers, and God now worked through this great new organism. And just as a bride needs time to prepare herself for her wedding day, so God is preparing His Church for the Marriage Supper of the Lamb. One day, the trumpet will sound and the Father will call the Bride for His Son.

But God hasn't forgotten His people, the Jews. Their final week hasn't yet taken place. Daniel writes of that final week in Daniel 9:27, "He shall confirm the covenant with many for one week (seven years): and in the midst of the week (seven years) he shall cause the sacrifice and the oblation to cease, and for the overspreading of abominations he shall make it desolate, even until the consummation, and that determined shall be poured upon the desolate."

The final seven or the final week of Daniel culminates in the abomination of desolation when the Son of Satan declares himself to be God.

Are you ready? The stopwatch could start at anytime. The signs are all around you but are you watching for them? Are you living your life in the light that God's time for the Church's rapture could come at any moment?

THE SEASON

Aside from the obvious reasons that there has been no greater evidence technologically speaking for the events of the Tribulation, I believe there are two main reasons the Rapture will happen soon.

Seven is God's perfect number. We know God created the earth in six days and on the seventh, He rested. This number is used over and over again in Scripture concerning prophecy. Second Peter 3:8 states, "But, beloved, be not ignorant of this one thing, that one day is with the Lord as a thousand years, and a thousand years as one day." God created time and delights in its order. To Him, one thousand years is as one day. We can't imagine this. Sometimes to us, one day seems like a thousand years. We know the Millennium period is one thousand years. This is the final thousand years of rest, representing the day God rested after Creation. Approximately two thousand years have gone by since Christ died. We know that about four thousand years had passed when Christ died. Add those together and you have seven thousand years. A perfect week. And a perfect way to end time forever.

But the Rapture should have already happened at about the year 2000 if this was God's ideal plan. Most prophecy

scholars felt that the Rapture would occur at the year 2000
or several years later because the calendar isn't perfect.
Except I've always felt that the Rapture wouldn't occur then.
Not when you look closely at Daniel's prophecy of seventy
sevens.

Daniel 9:25-26 explains, "Know therefore and
understand, that from the going forth of the commandment
to restore and to build Jerusalem unto the Messiah the Prince
shall be seven weeks, and threescore and two weeks: the
street shall be built again, and the wall, even in troublous
times. And after threescore and two weeks shall Messiah be
cut off, but not for himself: and the people of the prince that
shall come shall destroy the city and the sanctuary; and the
end thereof shall be with a flood, and unto the end of the war
desolations are determined."

After Jerusalem was built, there were 483 years until the
death of Christ. Then the parenthetical time period started.
I've always believed that the missing seven years will be
added directly to the 483 years of Daniel—as if the Church
age never happened. This would put the Rapture to the year
2007 plus or minus a few years depending by how off the
calendar is. Understand that I'm not setting a date, rather I'm
saying that if you look at God's perfect time and estimate
that His time has seven thousands in it, then the season for
the Rapture is most definitely now.

God's calendar for the Jews was exact. If you study
the Old Testament you will see close symmetry in the time
periods between major events. If the Jews were watching,
they could have predicted the year their Messiah would ride
into Jerusalem. We know the Tribulation period is the same
way, as each event will happen in perfect precision, just as
it was predicted. This is why the world is without excuse
when Jesus appears at the Second Coming. There has always
been evidence that God and His Son are real, but during the
Tribulation, the signs will be so apparent that every person
on the earth will be forced to make a decision either for or
against Christ.

As believers, we don't have that same luxury for prediction of the Rapture. Jesus told us that no man knows the day or the hour of His return. The Church Age is less defined in a sense. In some ways, it is still a mystery. But I still believe there is a perfection to God's timing, therefore we could well be at the end of this parenthetical time. Remember, I'm not a prophet, the son of a prophet, or even the nephew of a prophet. I'm certainly not predicting the exact time of the Rapture. That would be foolish. But in looking at how God loves order and always has a purpose to His timing, we can know the season. You do the math.

We will all be somewhat surprised by the Lord's coming, but we shouldn't be too surprised when we remember our Lord told us to watch and wait for His soon return.

READY OR NOT

Isaac Storm wrote a book about a storm that destroyed Galveston in 1900. Everyone was convinced that a hurricane could never strike Galveston, even as one approached. The author vividly describes how, as the streets began to flood, people went about their business as if nothing were wrong. Children played in the water, men gathered for breakfast at the local diner, and no one fled from the storm that was about to strike.

Some didn't worry because the national weather service officer in Galveston assured them it would not be a severe storm. Others simply believed Galveston was invincible. Some thought that since they had never seen a hurricane strike Galveston, one never would. For a number of reasons people assured themselves nothing bad would happen. As a result over 6,000 people died one September day in 1900.

Today we can see storm clouds forming on the horizon. There is a moral and spiritual decline that continues to erode our national life. The warning signs are there for us to see. They beckon us to return to the Lord and seek refuge in Him. However, some modern day prophets assure us there is nothing to fear, others believe this nation to be invincible, some think since they have never seen judgment it can't happen to them. How will history look back on what we did as the storm approached?

Jesus said we wouldn't know the day or the hour of His return, but that we would know the season. We would look around us and begin to understand that Satan is setting the world up for the time of his son.

FIRST THE RAPTURE

If you know the Lord as your Savior, then you can look forward to the Rapture. And you don't have to worry about recognizing or not recognizing the Antichrist.

That's because you will be gone.

The Bible says the Rapture is the event that signals the beginning of the Tribulation period. And if you have studied anything about this event then you will know that while it will be glorious for believers, it will be catastrophic for the rest of the world.

- Airplanes piloted by Christians will crash.
- Cars driven by believers suddenly will be driverless.
- Shopping centers and grocery stores will be thrown into a panic.
- Phones will be off the hook around the world.
- Computer centers and networks will crash.
- Millions of people will be missing, and no one will know why.
- Funerals will be disrupted.
- Some cemeteries will be free of corpses.
- There will be weeping, wailing, and gnashing of teeth.
- The world will be ready to accept anyone who can explain the catastrophe.
- They will be ripe for Satan's "I-will-ascend-above-the-Most-High" plan.

THE SON OF SATAN

He could already be waiting in the wings. He could be alive today. I know one thing for sure. Until the Rapture, the world won't know who he is.

As we delve into the study of this personification of humanism, remember the next great event on God's calendar: The Rapture of the Church. The Glorious Appearing. The Blessed Hope.

Will you be taken up? Do you know the Lord Jesus as your Savior? If so, then you won't ever have to meet this man. He won't deceive you. You won't have to take his mark to buy or sell. But your friends and family might. That's why we must tell them. We must tell everyone we know that the Son of Satan is about to appear on the scene. And we must tell them of God's great love . . . before it's too late.

THE REAL SIGN

Christ made repeated references to people being deceived by false teachers at the end. I believe this is one of the most compelling reasons the Rapture is close at hand. In Matthew 24, Jesus answered the disciples' questions about the end of the age by warning them about coming religious leaders seeking to mislead.

- "Take heed that no man deceive you" (Mat. 24:4).
- "For many shall come in my name, saying, I am Christ; and shall deceive many" (Mat. 24:5).
- "And many false prophets shall rise, and shall deceive many" (Mat. 24:11).
- "Then if any man shall say unto you, Lo, here is Christ, or there; believe it not" (Mat. 24:23).
- "For there shall arise false Christs, and false prophets, and shall shew great signs and wonders; insomuch that, if it were possible, they shall deceive the very elect" (Mat. 24:24).
- "Wherefore if they shall say unto you, Behold, he is

in the desert; go not forth: behold, he is in the secret
chambers; believe it not" (Mat. 24:26).

While there have been false teachers deceiving Christians
and the world from the first century A.D., there has never
been a time when false religion has been so prominent. We
have all heard of Jim Jones' followers in Guyana, in 1978;
David Koresh and the Branch Davidians in Texas, 1993; the
Heaven's Gate group in southern California, 1997; the recent
Raelian cult, and the list goes on. Just a search on Google
will turn up thousands of groups all over the world.

There are also false teachers who don't so blatantly
twist Scripture as the aforementioned cults do, but who use
the Bible to "justify" their teachings. They do "signs" and
"wonders," and many people are deceived. And yet, this is
just more proof of Christ's soon return.

A True Stradivari

The most famous violinmaker who has ever lived, Antonio
Stradivari, created more than 600 violins as well as many
cellos, violas, guitars, mandolins, and harps in his career.
Many violin makers tried to imitate this extraordinary
craftsman. In fact, many musical instruments of that era put
the word "Stradivarius" on their violins, although the true
Stradivari never touched them. How do collectors know what
a true Stradivari looks like? To this day, his work remains
unsurpassed. A genuine Stradivari violin almost always
features a belly of fine-grained spruce, with curly maple
back and sides. He created graceful musical instruments,
and he put his heart into every one he made. Of the 1,100
instruments he is believed to have created in his lifetime, 709
survive today. One of his violins recently sold at auction at
Christie's for $1,326,000.[5]

How will you know whether a prophet or a teacher is
teaching correctly? Because everything he or she says will
line up with Scripture. Just as a true expert knows when she
sees a real Stradivarius, so a true student of the Word knows

when the teacher is teaching the truth.

Know your Bible. Compare any teaching with the Word of God. If anything they teach contradicts Scripture, then you will be able to spot false teachers.

Ryan, a man in my church, came to know the Lord through a challenge. A man walked into his place of business wearing a t-shirt with a Bible verse on it. Ryan was totally against the Bible at the time. When he saw this customer, he felt extremely angry. He went to the man and told him to get out of his store. Somehow the man struck up a conversation with him finally challenging Ryan to get a Bible of his own and study it for himself. Ryan surprised even himself by doing just that. He started to read the Bible daily trying to understand what it meant. One day, he met another man who told him to listen to a certain show on the radio. Ryan decided to listen, and in a few months trusted Christ as his Savior. He ended up joining our church as a result of listening to *Victory In Grace*, the radio broadcast that man had told him about.

Ryan avoided falling into the trap of false teaching because he was grounded in the Word of God. You need to do the same thing. Make sure you understand God's Word enough to detect false teaching when you hear it or read it.

THE SIGN OF THE AGE

We look for the coming of the Lord mainly because there were certain signs predicted that just couldn't have happened years ago. Looking at our world today, we see a stunning set up for this coming world leader. We see a world that is more than capable of giving every person a mark without which he or she cannot buy or sell. We see a world where vast numbers of people take their views from CNN without ever leaving their armchairs. It is easy to imagine how this leader will steal the hearts of all people. Even in the poorest parts of India, the government provides televisions to the villages. Even people from remote areas will know about the Son of Satan. He will burst from obscurity to prominence in a matter of hours. Could there have been a better time in history for this to happen?

As we absorb our ever-growing, technologically changing culture, we see the signs of the end. The signs Jesus told His disciples to look for. The signs that Satan has one more plan up his sleeve—unleashing his personal clone, his personal embodiment, his personal slave.

The Son of Satan could be alive today. But you wouldn't know it was he . . . no one will . . . not until the appointed time.

CHAPTER 3

The Names

The Garden of Eden
Genesis 3

HE WISHED HE KNEW THE END FROM THE BEGINNING; IT WOULD REALLY HELP IN TIMES LIKE THIS. Instead, he had to sit back and wait, hoping he'd played his cards right, hoping he'd done everything he could to make sure his plan would work. And of course, it would work. However, sometimes he wondered. Those walking pseudo-angels seemed to have been programmed with a free will feature that even he didn't have. While they enjoyed a powerful, all-fulfilling walk with God, surely he could interest them in a different path.

He twisted slightly as he looked at the ground. He had deliberately chosen the most beautiful creature in the garden as his costume. It did him well, he thought, gave him some of his old sparkle. He knew she loved beautiful things. What with the way she scurried around collecting hyacinths, lilies, and orchids to line the place they slept, he knew she would be enamored with the colors of the serpent. Vivid, powerful, they glowed with the very essence of God's best. Today, he glowed with new life.

He was taking a risk—he knew that. Why anyone would want anything else besides this gorgeous place was past comprehension. Though he knew he was already past such thoughts himself.

That still small voice. He sensed it for a moment. He remembered when he had heard it and thrilled to its very essence. He remembered the Throne and the Glory. Watching them enjoy the Presence as he had once enjoyed it made him writhe with envy.

Enough of that. He deserved all the glory now. He saw them walking toward him, though of course they weren't aware that he was there, he brought the branches close to his body.

Blissful, their happiness shone from their pores. They were talking out loud with each other and with . . . Satan tensed, yes, they were talking with Him. Hatred poured out of him. Talking to God. Walking with Him. The couple's evident contentment only pressed him forward.

The man and woman seemed to cease speaking. Good. Satan forced himself to calm down. Whatever happened, he must not show anything but the purest delight in being a creation of God, at least for the moment.

She wandered on through, evidently searching for different flowers to add to her bouquet. It was time. Satan wondered ever so briefly if she would listen. If she could talk to God at a moment's notice, why would she bother talking to him?

Sudden pride filled his spirit. She would listen. Of course, she would. It was because of his startling beauty that she would stop and look, and look again. She would eat of the fruit. He'd noticed her looking at the tree the day before. He was counting on her temptation for the one thing she couldn't have. He had fallen for much the same reason.

He wrapped himself around the trunk, feeling the smooth bark beneath his skin. His plan was clearer than it had ever been. He would just ask her a question. The simplest of simple questions. She would answer, and before she knew it, she would do the same thing he had already done. Then she would talk to her husband. She would have to, for surely she could never talk to God again. She was almost past the tree. He opened his mouth and called her by name.

* *

IF ADAM AND EVE COULD HAVE KNOWN THE CHASM THEY WERE NEARING, THEY WOULD NEVER HAVE EVEN TALKED ABOUT THE WEATHER WITH THE SERPENT. If they could have fathomed in the smallest degree what their disobedience would do to not only them but to their children and children's children, they probably would have run as fast as they could past the snake.

However, there were no danger signs. No flashing lights, no ringing alarms. The couple had probably walked past the Tree of the Knowledge of Good and Evil many times. They might have said to each other as they gazed on it, "That's the tree we are never to eat. Let us never do such a thing! This garden is so beautiful that we want to do exactly what God says to do."

Their fellowship with God before the fall was sweet, fulfilling, and perfect. They had no need that wasn't met. There is no way to describe their complete happiness, their joy at possessing such a close walk with their Creator.

The warning to us today is that as believers, we are often at the same dangerous point as Adam and Eve that fateful day they talked to Satan. We don't realize how close we are to throwing our lives away for the briefest of pleasures.

I've written before about the Mr. or Mrs. Sin that all of us are prone toward. This weakness is the one that Old Serpent knows all about. We could be in the most innocent of places, a restaurant, a hotel room, a mall, even a church lobby and be tempted, just as Adam and Eve were tempted. Since the Old Serpent knows our weakness, he can sometimes be more effective with the temptation than we could ever realize beforehand.

If we would just stop and consider even now the repercussions of bowing to this sin, we would never think about committing it. If we ask God to show us when we are close to a danger point, then we can have the power to run away from such a temptation. We must constantly understand that we can do the wrong thing at a moment's notice. Don't put more blame at Adam and Eve's door than you would place at your own door. You and I are constantly bombarded with temptations, and many times we Christians don't react in the correct manner toward them.

Will you take a moment right now and ask God to show you an area in your life where Mr. or Mrs. Sin could reside if you let him? Will you confess your weakness toward that sin and ask God to give you the strength to flee such a temptation in the future? My friend, remember God is greater than any temptation you face, but you must appropriate that power for it to be effective in your life. As we continue to understand our own weaknesses and tendencies, we learn to depend more wholly on our great God.

SWINDLED BY AN ANIMAL

The Scriptures record that Eve talked willingly to what she thought was just an animal. She didn't hesitate or ask why an animal was speaking to her. I'm sure Adam and Eve were constantly amazed by God's incredible creativity since Creation, so this was probably just some new phenomenon to her. She replied, never dreaming that someone was trying to ruin her and her husband's lives. The Bible says Adam was also there with her and yet, there is no record that he said anything to the Serpent. He didn't try to stop Eve from eating the fruit, and when she offered it to him, he ate it willingly.

Adam and Eve obviously didn't understand how great their dominion was, given to them from Almighty God. They should have realized that they could have stood up to what was happening and said, "Get out of here, Serpent! We are not going to talk to someone who tells us to go against our God." Instead, it seems they almost didn't stop to think—instead they reacted without thinking.

Pastor of Moody Church, Erwin Lutzer, makes an interesting point about this. He wrote, "Adam and Eve deceived by an animal! They had the authority to expel this creature from the garden; they could have banished him from the face of the earth. They could have taken their God-given dominion seriously and said no to the creature's whims. All that, yet they foolishly acted on his suggestions! Birds, fish, and creeping things—all these were under man's authority. The serpent that showed up uninvited in their garden and now spoke to them so compassionately—this beast was subject to Adam's command. Incredibly, Adam was seduced by a creature who was beneath him. He withdrew from his God-given responsibility and accepted the word of a beast. Man, who could have walked tall among the creatures, now stoops to the suggestion of one of them.

"Adam dropped the scepter, and Satan picked it up. Man, created to be king of the earth, would become a slave."[1]

Lutzer's observation is helpful to us if we learn to apply the lesson Adam and Eve learned to our own lives. As Christians, we don't always understand how great our God is; we don't always understand that we can denounce temptation with authority. In our own flesh, we have no power over temptation, but with the Spirit of God helping us, we can run away from it.

Perhaps you are feeling convicted about a temptation that keeps coming to you. Maybe you haven't given in yet, but you feel like you might soon. I ask you to understand that the Holy Spirit dwells within you. When you rely on His strength, you can learn to conquer sin. Just as Adam and Eve had the authority given to them by the Almighty God to banish the Serpent from the Garden when he first started making them question the Lord, so you have the authority to say no to temptation. Remember Hebrews 2:18 in times like this, "For in that he himself hath suffered being tempted, he is able to succor [or give relief to] them that are tempted."

Why don't you spend some time in prayer right now and ask God to help you do this? He has promised to give you both strength and help . . . right when you need it.

THE GLITTERING SERPENT

Satan purposefully wanted them to sin so he could win. He found that his own plans would come back to haunt him. He thought Adam and Eve would be banished just as he was; and he was right, they were. He thought Adam and Eve would know good and evil just as he did; and he was right, they did. He thought Adam and Eve would die physically and spiritually just as he did. This was where he was wrong. Their physical flesh would die, but God would provide an antidote for their spirits. God was a God of justice, but He was also a God of mercy. One day, God's own Son would come and die for the sins of the world. All who trust Him are given eternal life. Satan's plan played right into the hands of the all-knowing, all-powerful God.

One day, Satan will deceive the world using a glittering serpent disguised as the Antichrist. Instead of wrapping himself around the tree, the Antichrist will announce that he has the answers, that if all would follow him, everybody will be prosperous beyond their wildest dreams. Sadly, many people will listen and be deceived just as Eve was. Yet, we see God's redeeming grace as the Antichrist in the end brings the world to its final judgment. The world will then look on Jesus Christ, whom they have pierced, and will be forced to give obeisance to Him.

THE HERETIC

When we study the names of the Antichrist in Scripture, we begin to understand more about his coming nature. One of those names of Antichrist is "heretic." What is a heretic? Someone who holds to unorthodox beliefs. The Apostle John could probably have brought out many false teachings of the Antichrist but he chose to focus on one in particular—Christology, that is the study of Christ. When an antichrist would come, one way to tell if he or she was real or not was what they believed about Christ. If their doctrine of Christ was warped, specifically they didn't believe Jesus was the Son of God, come in the flesh, and as fully God as God Himself, then they were not of Christ. Every cult denies this truth. First John 2:22 states, "Who is a liar but he that denieth that Jesus is the Christ? He is antichrist, that denieth the Father and the Son."

There have been and still are many antichrists. These are men and women who have come and said, "I am the Christ" but then their words and actions speak of anything but. This was one of the ways we were told we would be able to know we were coming to the end of the age.

Just as the Serpent deceived Eve in the Garden of Eden, so a glittering Serpent will deceive the world with a single question:

Why should we not all be like God?

To the New Ager, the question isn't too far from many people's current beliefs. For aren't we all little gods? it is said. Isn't everything we do godlike? Can't we, if enough of us believe it, possess godlike powers? The faulty logic continues, why can't we just be God? In the end, such deadly reasoning continues until man has built his own Tower of Babel spiraling to the sky.

KNOWN BY HIS OPPOSITE NATURE

Every one of the Antichrist's names mentioned in the Bible signifies satanic power. Every title describes his subtleness, his corrupt nature, and his deceitful heart. What Satan is in spirit form, he will be in human flesh. His thoughts, motivations and actions will be against God to the exaltation of Satan.

Look at Daniel 7:25, "And he shall speak great words against the most High, and shall wear out the saints of the most High, and think to change times and laws: and they shall be given into his hand until a time and times and the dividing of time."

Look for a moment at some of the differences between Christ and Satan.

- Christ was the man of Sorrows—The Antichrist shall be the Man of Sin.
- Christ was the Perfect One—The Antichrist shall be the Lawless One.

- Christ is the King of Kings—The Antichrist shall be the Willful King and King of Babylon.
- Christ is the Lamb—The Antichrist shall be the Beast.

THE MAN OF SIN

Think about this title: "the man of sin." Second Thessalonians 2:3 explains, "Let no man deceive you by any means: for that day shall not come, except there come a falling away first, and that man of sin be revealed, the son of perdition."

All that is sinful, all that is vile, and all that is unrighteous is invested in its fullness in the Son of Satan. Sin is running rampant today, yet there is a control, a limit put there by the Holy Spirit. However, when the Antichrist comes on the scene everything will be a "go." Nothing will be restrained; every vice will have its freedom, as it will be centered in him. Sin will not be restrained in any manner, for he will lead the world in the basest of sinful conduct.

Professor Mark Cambron wrote, "Whatever sin can be named, he will practice it, for he is the Man of Sin, not merely a sinner but the embodiment of all that which is unholy, debased, and amoral."[2]

This isn't a man you would want to meet in either a dark alley or a lighted corner, for he is so good at sinning that he appears eminently good.

THE LIAR

Second Thessalonians 2:11 tells us more about this coming man's lying nature. "And for this cause God shall send them strong delusion, that they should believe a lie."

Have you ever known someone who lied so much that he believed his own lies? Throughout the years, I've known a few people like that, and they are particularly dangerous to other people. Why? Because they can look someone in the eye and assure him that what they are saying is true. They are so used to lying, it is such a way of life for them that they believe everything they say. They believe their lies so strongly that it is often difficult for even a close friend or a spouse to see that they are lying.

Years ago, we had a boy in our Christian school who was like this. He lied continually, and we prayed and hoped that one day he would see the error of his ways. One day, several of his teachers brought him into my office. There were many proofs that he had been shoplifting, and each of these proofs was laid out before the boy. Remarkably, he continued to insist that he had nothing to do with the theft. It was almost humorous, in a sad way. I remember thinking as I looked into that boy's eyes that unless he understood his lying nature, he would never make it in his Christian life.

The Antichrist will take lying to a different dimension than that boy. He will be such a liar that no one will believe he is one. He will look his followers in the eye and cause them to believe him. He will then launch the ultimate lie, that he, himself, is the Christ, the perfect One and demand abject worship.

All this will come slowly, so people won't suspect. They will believe the ultimate lie because of their strong desire for peace. Before they know it, war of catastrophic proportions will come upon their heads. Their willingness to believe the lie of the Antichrist will cause them to endure suffering greater than any suffering the world has ever known.

The Willful King

The Antichrist is called the Willful King of Babylon. His will is Satan's will. Daniel 11:36 explains, "And the king shall do according to his will; and he shall exalt himself, and magnify himself above every god, and shall speak marvelous things against the God of gods, and shall prosper till the indignation be accomplished: for that that is determined shall be done."

In Revelation chapters 17 and 18, we learn about Babylon being built again. This is the Revived Roman Empire during the first half of the 70th week of Daniel. The Antichrist will rule the One-World Church and the One-World Government. He will be its King.

THE LITTLE HORN AND THE BEAST

We will delve more into this later as we study the events of the Tribulation period. For now, read Revelation 17:11, "And the beast that was, and is not, even he is the eighth, and is of the seven, and goeth into perdition."

THE SON OF PERDITION AND THE LAWLESS ONE

Judas was called the Son of Perdition. Of course, we all know what Judas did when he betrayed our Lord. The Antichrist will have Judas' sordid attributes. He will not be a "reincarnated" Judas, as some would teach, but he will betray the Lord in the same way as Judas Iscariot did.

The Antichrist is also called the Lawless One. His lawlessness is reflected in the fact that he will seem to be carefully following every law even as he changes them and creates new ones that cater to his huge ego. He will break all of God's laws and cause men to do likewise.

THE ANTICHRIST

Why is the Antichrist called the Antichrist? The word "antichrist" from the Greek means "an opponent of Messiah," but just because he is against Christ doesn't mean that he will seem to be against Christ. He will do many things that mimic Christ, which will be one of the key ways he deceives his followers.

First John 2:18 tells us more about this Antichrist: "Little children, it is the last time: and as ye have heard that antichrist shall come, even now are there many antichrists; whereby we know that it is the last time."

Why are there many antichrists before the final Antichrist will come? The Bible says these people are a sign that the final days are close upon us. From false prophets to our modern day false teachers who shroud the truth and tell lies to their followers, all these people are merely predecessors of the final Antichrist.

Satan will present this mock christ to the world as its

savior, friend, and redeemer. First John 4:3-4 explains more, "And every spirit that confesseth not that Jesus Christ is come in the flesh is not of God: and this is that spirit of antichrist, whereof ye have heard that it should come; and even now already is it in the world. Ye are of God, little children, and have overcome them: because greater is he that is in you, than he that is in the world."

Take heart, dear friend. Even as we now look around us and see many who have fallen away from the truth, many who teach a false message, so we see the Bible clearly tells us that the Holy Spirit is greater than any antichrist.

Do you feel worried about those who are against the truth? There is no need to fret. Stay true to God and His Word. Remember the Holy Spirit is inside you, and He is so much greater than any false teacher that it defies description.

HELD IN RESERVE

If the Antichrist is alive today, he is not in the limelight at present. He is being kept in reserve until the rapture takes place. Then he shall rise as a Middle East diplomat, as a problem-solver solving many delicate problems in the world today, especially those things pertaining to the nation of Israel.

My old college professor, Dr. Mark Cambron, said this about the Antichrist: "By his own manipulations success after success will follow him until first a rumor of him is heard, then a roar of his popularity is recognized and finally his name will be a household word."[3]

I remember a story about a man who while visiting a certain school made a promise to the students that he would give a prize to the one whose desk was found in the best order when he returned. He gave no indication of when that might be. Shortly after he left, a little girl, noted for her messy habits, announced that she meant to win that prize.

Her classmates jeered, "Why, Mary, your desk is always out of order! It's never been cleaned."

"Oh," she replied, "Starting right now, I'm going to clean

it up the first of every week."

"Just suppose he comes at the end of the week?"

"Well then, I'll clean it every morning."

"What if he comes in the afternoon?"

Mary was silent, then her face lit up and she said, "I know what I'll do, I'll just keep it clean all the time!"

That's how we should live as believers. Ready all the time for the trumpet sound.

Are you ready? Are you beginning to understand the importance of serving the Lord with your whole heart? Are you starting to see why you should live your life prepared for our Lord's soon return? Take a moment to pray this prayer: *Lord, help me to be ready for Your return. Help me to keep Your soon return in my mind as I go about my daily business. Help me to live with the reality of Your coming and help that awareness to transform my life.*

Keep waiting, watching, and praying. The anticipation of Jesus' soon return will bring joy to your Christian walk.

CHAPTER 4

The Conceit

The Courts of Heaven
Job 1:6-12

"HE IS ONLY GOOD BECAUSE YOU ARE SO GOOD TO HIM," SATAN HAD BEEN GRANTED ACCESS TO GOD, AND HE WANTED TO MAKE FULL USE OF HIS TIME. He had been tempting the sons and daughters of men with good results, but while most giddily did what he said, not all listened.

The Voice was calm, measured. "There is none greater than my servant, Job."

Satan hated the words "my servant" more than any others. How could any mortal dare to defy his authority and obey the Creator—seeming to want to lay his life before the Throne?

He brought his hands together. "You do not know that Job is great because of what he has or because of his love for you."

"He is my servant. I have blessed him, but he is not dependent on those blessings."

Satan remembered his own blessings at the beginning, how he had shaken them off when he fell through the Heavens. And yet, some humans seemed to love God on their own, even as they sometimes obeyed his own commands scurrying to yield to his temptations. He remembered watching Job gather with his family the night before.

"Come my children," Job called, "Before you go to your own homes to feast, I have something to say to you."

Quite a diverse group gathered around the man. The

children were all in their forties. The tallest son was known as the strong one, the second as the handsome one, the third as the shrewd one. The three sisters all shared dark, lustrous hair and green eyes. Known for their beauty, they had their choice of the men in the land for husbands. Yet, they were waiting for their father's advice. They seemed content in this.

Satan had tried to tempt each of the children to go against their father, and none of them wanted to listen to him either. Job seemed to have given them much of his own God-given wisdom.

Job's wisdom also irritated him. The man knew how to please God. He not only offered sacrifices every morning for his own sin, but he offered them up for his children as well. The sweet smell of the burning reached the Heavens.

I deserve the praise, Satan thought. *I deserve the sacrifices.*

But, how was he going to get to Job? He didn't seem to want to listen to him as Eve had, as so many of the sons of men had. He seemed to enjoy the voice of God the most.

Satan watched as Job blessed each of his children, holding them close and praying over them. He wanted to breathe fire in their faces. Instead, he had to watch. For God had restrained his hands.

He wanted to raise his fist to the sky, but for the moment he didn't dare. He might have tried to tempt Job and his children, but God had put an invisible wall around everything Job possessed. Every time he went to torment Job, he hit it.

He growled. If he could only get through, if he could only torment Job by taking away his riches, then he could win.

He needed access. He hated to do it because it seemed so beneath him, but his need to hurt was greater than his own pride.

That was why he was standing in the outer courts of Heaven today. God almost seemed to enjoy his anger.

The verdict came. "Go ahead. Take all that he has."

His heart leaped.

"But, don't touch his body. You are not allowed to harm him."

He bristled at the words. Imagine, God giving him orders! He disappeared, not wanting to show his anger, afraid God would bring back the protective hedge.

I will destroy him by taking his home, his cattle, and his tents, he thought. Then, he stopped. He remembered the scene the night before. He thought about Job's face as he looked at his children.

No, I will destroy them too. His children mean more to him than his other blessings.

He hovered over the home, gazing appreciatively at all the man possessed.

Job, prepare to curse God with me.

* *

SATAN WANTS PURE AUTHORITY IN EVERY LIFE. That is why he brings the Man of Sin forward to deceive the world. But Job withstood the destruction Satan brought upon him. It must have irritated Satan to see Job continue to bless the Lord even as he was stripped of everything he possessed. Though many human beings had bowed to Satan, the Devil wanted this man who refused. Satan wasn't content with what he had—he is never content! The Devil always wants more of everything, and nothing delights him more than to sabotage a servant of the Lord. He understands that a true servant of the Lord has many people who look up to him or her. He knows the scope of his or her influence. If he causes that man or woman to turn away from God, then he wreaks havoc far and wide.

Remember, dear one, the more you serve the Lord and the less you yield to Satan, the more his desire to destroy you will increase. This shouldn't scare you as much as it should put you on guard.

Think about Job and how he withstood the attacks, never even knowing where the attacks were coming from.

Consider how Satan tempted David to number Israel in 1 Chronicles 21. His intent was to bring David down, so that all of Israel would be brought down. We know Satan tempted the Apostle Paul (2 Cor. 12:7), and we can see that he did it for much the same reason as he tempted other great leaders in the Bible.

Managing Editor of *Christian History* magazine, Chris Armstrong writes about the famous theologian Jonathan Edwards in *Leadership Journal.* He says Edwards faced incredible opposition in his own church that led to his eventual dismissal. Armstrong writes,

> As messy dismissals of ministers go, the 1750 ejection of Jonathan Edwards by his Northampton congregation was among the messiest. . . . Friends and enemies alike agreed that in the long, sinking discontent, Edwards continued to love and pray for—or at least tolerate and refrain from attacking—his people, even when they bared their fangs.
>
> Salary controversies and power struggles marked his ministry during the 1740's. In the infamous "bad book" episode of 1744, some teen boys in the church distributed a midwife's manual, using it to taunt and make "suggestive comments" in front of girls.
>
> When the culprits were summoned before the church, their response, according to documents of the proceedings, was "contemptuous . . . toward the authority of this Church."[1]

Then Edwards' uncle, Colonel John Stoddard, died in 1748. The colonel was a sharp thinker, a county judge, and a savvy politician. He sat under Edwards' ministry Sunday after Sunday. Edwards leaned on Stoddard's influence to navigate the affairs of the church, but when he died it was open season among others in the congregation.

Edwards' cousin, Israel Williams, was a Harvard graduate

who hated Edwards. Williams served as a counselor and ringleader of Edwards' opposition. Then Edwards insisted that all people who wanted to join the church must "make a public profession of godliness" and the church revolted, eventually asking him to resign, which he did. Edwards moved his family to Massachusetts where he continued to labor for the Lord, writing many famous theological works including his biography of David Brainerd.

As we think about the opposition Edwards faced, we can only say that Satan was behind it. He thought he could ruin Edwards by forcing him out of his church and yet, we see Edwards' incredible faith as he continued to serve the Lord. How that faith must have grated on Satan as he watched Edwards' faithfulness in spite of all that he brought upon him.

How to Stay Faithful

Job's continued service—in spite of losing his seven sons and three daughters as well as his wealth—grated on Satan, too. He went back to the Lord and asked to afflict his body, convinced that personal, physical pain would cause Job to curse God. Even Job's wife asked Job to curse God at this point in Job 2:9-10, "Then said his wife unto him, Dost thou still retain thine integrity? Curse God, and die. But he said unto her, Thou speakest as one of the foolish women speaketh. What? shall we receive good at the hand of God, and shall we not receive evil? In all this did not Job sin with his lips."

Imagine if that line could be written about us! Think about what it would be like to endure severe hardship like Job experienced and still not sin with our lips. Many people have a tendency to sin with their lips when the smallest thing goes wrong.

Read what Job says in 1:21, "And said, Naked came I out of my mother's womb, and naked shall I return thither: the Lord gave, and the Lord hath taken away; blessed be the name of the Lord."

Job endured his wife telling him to curse the Lord;

he tolerated three of his friends who supposedly came to comfort him but instead spent most of their time blaming Job for what had happened to him. In the end, Job doesn't curse God, but he does question Him. However, the beauty of it is, at the rebuke of the Lord, Job fell on his face and confessed his sin.

What a beautiful picture of our own walk as believers. We are going to be tempted by Satan, our friends are going to forsake us, and we will sometimes question God even as Job did. We are told that if we confess our sin, God is faithful to forgive us (1 John 1:9).

God ended up giving Job more than he had possessed in the beginning of the story. Job 42:12-17 explains, "So the Lord blessed the latter end of Job more than his beginning: for he had fourteen thousand sheep, and six thousand camels, and a thousand yoke of oxen, and a thousand she asses. He had also seven sons and three daughters. And he called the name of the first, Jemima; and the name of the second, Kezia; and the name of the third, Keren-happuch. And in all the land were no women found so fair as the daughters of Job: and their father gave them inheritance among their brethren. After this lived Job an hundred and forty years, and saw his sons, and his sons' sons, even four generations. So Job died, being old and full of days."

Dear friend, you too are going to face the opposition of Satan. You too will be tempted. This will happen more and more as we await the coming of the Lord. Will you ask the Lord right now to help you continue to serve Him in spite of the temptation? Will you go before the Lord believing that He is holding you in the palm of His hand, that He is greater than any dart Satan can throw? He will shelter you and uphold you, even as you face hardships and difficulties. What a blessed promise from our Lord. I encourage you to thank Him for that promise right now.

OPPOSITION 101

Why is Satan not totally successful in his quest to conquer

the human race and turn them all away from God? We know from Scripture that the Holy Spirit indwells believers. The Holy Spirit also convicts the world of sin, unrighteousness, and judgment. This influence keeps evil from becoming more rampant than it already is. This influence keeps some control in the world.

This is why the world will be so ripe for total evil when the trumpet sounds and Christians rise at the rapture. No longer will there be much influence for good in this world. God will still be in control, but He tells us these coming seven years will be worse than any the world has ever known.

Even during that time, many people trust Christ as Savior. They will see events happening day by day that are perfectly outlined in Scripture. These events will bring those who are seeking the Lord hard evidence to believe God.

So understand that even as Satan struggles for supremacy, he ends up unable to do more than be a catalyst for events in God's timeline. It has to be the ultimate irony for Satan that everything he does only furthers God's plans. This doesn't mean God wishes to harm people or bring destruction on the world, in fact, the existence of prophecy shows His mercy. Why? Because He warns us of what is to come, and He gives every person a way out of the destruction to come. He sent His own Son to pay for the sins of the world, and every person who trusts in that payment is assured Heaven for all eternity.

Even as Satan brings forth this Deceiver, the Antichrist, he is simply fulfilling the Holy Scripture.

THE CONCEIT

What will be the main motivation for the Antichrist's deceit? His own ego and pride will drive him to the point that he allows Satan to control his every thought and movement. We saw Satan's pride as he told God, "It is only because you have given him so much that Job continues to bless you." Satan didn't want to think that people could simply love God for who He is and not for what He has given them.

It was also Satan's pride that made him say, "I will ascend into the Heavens. I will be like the most High," as recorded in Ezekiel. The world will witness his pride in a phenomenal way during the Tribulation period.

One day, the Antichrist will show the ultimate conceit; he will declare himself to be God. He will demand total worship and total allegiance. Sometimes we wonder how that might happen with so many countries suffering today from being ruled by ruthless dictators. However, imagine a dictator who doesn't seem like one. Think about what could happen if instead of a tyrant rising up by sheer force and brutality, he rose up with a pseudo-peace, an ability to unite the world with his cunning. His Satanic powers will enable him to pull the biggest swindle in the history of the world, because the world will believe he is a peace-loving man. Because of their overwhelming desire for peace, they will follow.

Second Thessalonians 2:4 explains more about the Antichrist's pride. "Who opposeth and exalteth himself above all that is called God, or that is worshipped; so that he as God sitteth in the temple of God, shewing himself that he is God." The ultimate conceit? The Antichrist will believe that he is not only greater than God; he is God.

THE FALSE PROPHET

Every evil dictator has someone who handles the propaganda side of things. Joseph Goebbels served in that role for Adolph Hitler when the Nazis came to power. Goebbels was a brilliant orator and one of the original spin-doctors who won quite a bit of Hitler's early popularity. Goebbel's only concern was to promote Hitler's viewpoint. And so it will be with the False Prophet. What are some of the False Prophet's earmarks?

Revelation 13:11-14 explains,

> And I beheld another beast coming up out of the earth; and he had two horns like a lamb, and he spake as a dragon. And he exerciseth all the power of the

first beast before him, and causeth the earth and them which dwell therein to worship the first beast, whose deadly wound was healed. And he doeth great wonders, so that he maketh fire come down from heaven on the earth in the sight of men, And deceiveth them that dwell on the earth by the means of those miracles which he had power to do in the sight of the beast; saying to them that dwell on the earth, that they should make an image to the beast, which had the wound by a sword, and did live.

The second beast described here will be the False Prophet. His ability to communicate with the masses will give all power to the first beast, which is the Antichrist. Think about the characteristics of the False Prophet in these verses. He has two horns "like a lamb," which means he will appear gentle like a lamb. He will probably use the lamb comparison saying he is like the "Lamb of God." This is simply a mask of his true intentions, for he will speak like a dragon.

In the long line at a tax office in Amman, Jordan, stood a man with a long white beard and a traditional headdress. Despite his face printed on the country's bank notes and stamps, no one recognized King Abdullah of Jordan, so ordinary was his disguise. King Abdullah had showed up with his half-brother Prince Ali to submit a bogus tax form. The king mentioned later that he enjoyed disguising himself so he could see how state-run agencies were doing and how they could improve.[2]

Of course, King Abdullah's intention for putting on ordinary clothing was not to deceive with the intention to hurt, but rather to help people. The False Prophet will deceive, coming in like a gentle zephyr, only to blast and kill with the fire of his devotion to the Antichrist.

He will be glad to say the words Satan wants him to say, using his brilliance as an orator to further the Antichrist's regime. He will bring the spiritual aspect into the reign, a culmination of all the world's religions, using the lingo people are used to hearing from their religious leaders.

He will have more power than Goebbels or any other oppressor's right hand man, for he will be able to do miracles. He will even be able to call fire down from Heaven just as the two witnesses in Revelation 11 will do. Consider for a moment how these signs and wonders will deceive many people. They will be real; the signs and wonders will be performed with bona fide satanic power. They won't be like many of the purported signs and wonders today, where simple investigation raises doubts as to their authenticity. Think about the unsaved people you know and the oppressed people who long for peace and security. These wonders will seem like the final reason to believe in the Antichrist, and they will seal the fate of thousands of people who then willingly take his mark.

The false prophet will build a fantastic image and cause it to speak. Imagine the news coverage of such an event: "The Miraculous Statue Speaks," "Thousands Observe Image Coming to Life," "Scientists Confirm Statue's Miracle" are some of the news headlines that could run about such an event. The image will probably be in the likeness of the Antichrist and will be in the spirit of the image Nebuchadnezzer built in Babylon. Think about the splendor and the build up for this ceremony. Consider all the hype television stations give for the Super Bowl and then think about all the buildup for this "miraculous" event.

Yesterday, none of us could have imagined that cloning technology would be a viable option. None of us could have thought robots could be created who could substitute for humans in battle. We couldn't have imagined the acceleration of technology to the point that this event in Scripture would be plausible to any person reading today.

And yet, Scripture again proves itself by predicting events and technologies that were not thought possible by people living a mere 100 years ago. Who would have thought that we could read about the False Prophet causing an image to speak and think that this could happen?

Doesn't this excite you as a believer to think about the authenticity of our Bible? It should cause us to appreciate anew our great God's revelation to us. It should cause you to leap for joy to think that you have Scripture you can trust. He knows the end from the beginning, and just in case we needed another proof, He tells us about an image that will speak and fool the world.

THE PUNISHMENT

Not only will people worship this image because it speaks, but also because the false prophet will kill "as many as would not worship the image of the beast." We see today many dictators who have done the same thing. We know Saddam Hussein called out members of his own Baath party during a public ceremony seemingly at random. Twenty-two people were condemned then marched out before all those Saddam had assembled. They were shot, bringing fear we can only imagine to all others who would dare to take power from Hussein. The message was clear: the smallest disagreement will be punished by death.

Dictators have to function this way. They can't allow dissension, for that means their power is in danger. The False Prophet and the Antichrist will bring this arrogant attitude to a new plane. As they march people out to kill them, people will believe that their brothers and sisters, mothers, and fathers deserved to die. They won't see the deadly deception until it is too late.

THE SPIRIT OF NEBUCHADNEZZAR

Consider again the amazing analogies of Scripture. Even while the False Prophet builds and demands worship of the Antichrist image, those who know the Old Testament, but don't know Christ (some archaeologists, the Jewish people, even liberal Bible scholars), cannot miss the resemblance of this event to one that happened during Nebuchadnezzar's reign. This incident and many of the others preceding it will probably cause them to study their Bibles where they will find the prophecies of Daniel, Christ, and Revelation happening before their eyes. They will hardly need faith like we do now to believe that Almighty God is indeed the only true God.

We know that later in the Tribulation period, 144,000 Jewish evangelists will win thousands upon thousands to Christ. The seeds will be planted as each event of the tribulation period fulfills itself to its ultimately horrifying potential.

Dear friend, do not fear the study of Bible prophecy. Instead, look at the study as an opportunity to acquaint yourself with the all-powerful hand of God. He is not a God Who enjoys bringing these events to pass; rather He has given us all these signs and prophecies of the last days to wake us up. He is the God of justice, but He is also the God of mercy. If He didn't care about the human race, all of these terrible events would happen without any warning. One reason prophecy figures so prominently in Scripture is so we can have more evidence for our faith. We can know God loves people so much that He reveals to them what will happen so that they will know He is real.

Tim LaHaye, co-author of the famous *Left Behind,* series says, "God does love this world! Bible prophecy proves it! … Amazing treasures await those who plunge into the world of Bible prophecy. For there we learn that if the Scriptures teach us anything about God, it's that He is for us. He is not against us!"[3]

It's true. Amazing treasures do await us as we study Bible prophecy. We learn more about God's nature and His Son, Jesus Christ. We discover that He is a God Who is bringing signs to pass so people have no excuse. As we study the prophecies still to come, we understand that God is showing us the seasons of those coming prophecies. He has given us even more reason to live righteous lives, telling others of the good news of His Son, sharing our joy with fellow believers, and continuing to read and study His Word.

Understand that we didn't need more reasons. The prophecies concerning the First Advent would have been enough. However, now the whole world is really without excuse. One day every eye will look upon Jesus Christ, whom they have pierced and they will mourn, as they should have mourned when He died. God is preparing the world for that day, wanting to draw as many to Himself as possible. This exciting truth of prophecy should cause you to leap for joy.

CHAPTER 5

The Humanist

Jerusalem
1 Chronicles 21:1

HE REMEMBERED IMPRESSIONS WHEN THE STONE HIT. Surprise more than shock. Fear because he didn't know if the giant was really dead or not. Then the giant's mouth twisted in surprise as he crashed to the earth. It would become the most talked-about battle in all of history.

Hundreds of able-bodied men had refused the challenge. Then today, one man, hardly more than a boy, marched out onto the field, determination his mantle. How could anyone know what fueled him? Insanity? Were his eyes failing him? Had he not seen how large that giant was? Did David really think he could win? Did he trust God that much?

He trusted God too much for Satan's peace of mind. It was the only way to explain the victory. Israelites, once timid but now empowered, ran out into the field and defeated their enemies. How David cut through that thick neck, Satan never knew but there David was, swinging the grotesque head around by its coarse hair. A victory for all. A personal victory for David. A glimmer of all that was to come.

Satan shifted. If David had known the trials he would go through, he might not have rested so easily that night.

Years in the wilderness. The most powerful man in Israel wanted him dead. David would live by his wits, sleeping on the cold, hard ground, eating whatever he could find, slowly building up a force of men who loved him and fought with him. Through it all, David could often be found outside the camp, strumming on his harp, singing songs. A musician.

Satan drew himself up. He hated David's musical gift. He didn't want to remember the beautiful music he had once crafted for the Creator. David's ability made Satan restless, anxious to tempt him. With every eager song that poured from his lips, Satan hated him more. God wouldn't let him touch him then. He grated his teeth.

Now he could. Satan had permission. He wanted to spit toward the Heavens in defiance at having to get consent, but he didn't dare. Right now it was time for ruin.

Satan sat outside the palace, considering how he would tempt David. He was tired of David's obedience, tired of unfailing devotion, tired of David winning the victory because of his total dependence on God.

Satan knew one thing. David had fought many battles, and he was weary. Exhausted all the way to the inner part of his marrow. That was why he welcomed the victory over the Philistines with such fervor.

Tonight David was going to throw a huge celebration. Servants dashed in and out of the doors getting supplies, buying fresh meat and bringing in baskets of flowers for decorations. The celebration would honor David's armies. They had rooted out the rest of Goliath's family members and killed them, no small feat, as these men came out of the same mold as the great giant himself. Before the battle, David's own nephew, Jonathan, had taken on the biggest one, the son, who had echoed the words of his father, "I defy the armies of Israel this day; give me a man, that we may fight together."

Jonathan had heard the story of his courageous uncle many times and now those words inspired him to stand against the giant and kill him. All of the relatives were slain that day, and David had received the news with great joy. The death of Goliath had been a touchstone in his life, now his nephew and militia continued the glory.

It was a day of unprecedented celebration. Word was all over Jerusalem that David had written a special Psalm of praise that he would share during the celebration.

The Psalm will take on a life of its own, sung over and over again, Satan thought, *I will tempt him before he plays his new Psalm.* Satan watched as torches were lit around town. He saw noblemen and warriors being escorted into David's residence. His eyes narrowed. David had too much influence. People followed him with their heart and soul. They loved him with an unbreakable love.

A thought came. Yes. He knew what he would do. The fact of this celebration could be the way to get to David. If there was ever a moment when David could be tempted to trust in his own strength, it was right now.

Somehow David needed to take his eyes off the Creator and look to himself, almost like Satan himself did that day when he had defied God. What if he put the thought into David's head that it wasn't God who had helped David, but indeed it was David himself who had been able to train men and an army with the capability to fight? David had worked hard, the spiraling reasoning could go, and he had given much. He had sacrificed. He had handled many crises and hardships. He had endured his own people blaming him for the enemy taking their wives and children. He had endured his own wives and children being taken.

He would ask David to number Israel. Surely, at this moment, David wouldn't see the harm in that. As a king, it was his right to know how many people were under his reign. Focus on the gift, rather than the Giver. The reasoning had worked with Eve. Instead of looking at the fact that it was God Who created food for her in the first place, she focused on the one command not to eat of a certain tree.

He would create the need. He hoped David would want to fill it.

* *

GOD'S CHASTISEMENT OF DAVID FOR NUMBERING ISRAEL WAS METED OUT SWIFTLY. Given three options for punishment,

David chose three days of pestilence for all of Israel. Remember, God works contrary to worldly thinking. This is demonstrated over and over in the Bible. The world says, "Swim with the culture, do what everyone else is doing," while God says, "Don't let the world squeeze you into its mold." Society shouts, "Fight and claw your way to the top of the ladder," while God says, "The meek shall inherit the earth." Some would tell us to count our resources, know how much we have so we can face whatever we need to face. On the other hand, Jesus told us to take no thought of tomorrow, rather we should be prepared to do whatever it is He wants us to do.

It was humanistic thinking Satan used on David. Know your resources, know how much you have. Know yourself. Films and videos consistently end with the message that it is only within oneself that there are answers to life's most perplexing problems. While we as Christians know that isn't true, we struggle just the same not to let that idea become our philosophy.

Does this mean we are never to plan for the future? Of course not. But, there is a clear biblical principle that ultimately David chose to ignore. It's a temptation that the coming Son of Satan will give in to completely. Scripture states that the heart is deceitful and desperately wicked. The only answers that can come from within us would be deceitful and wicked.

Satan desired David to rely on his own strength. He knew if he could turn David's eyes away from God, he would have the victory. He knew David resisted what we would today call "humanism," and he knew the only way to get David to sin was to turn his eyes from God to himself.

HUMANISM'S SPIRIT

One day, there will come a man in whom this spirit of humanism exists to an unprecedented degree. Our society has sheltered, taught, and embraced this philosophy more and more in the last few years, and this Man of Sin will embody the spirit of human reliance. Late Bible teacher, Ray Stedman notes of humanism and the coming Antichrist, "This idolatry of man has been building up throughout the centuries and is rapidly approaching the crisis when it will manifest itself, as the Lord describes in a clear symbol of the times. ... There is the empty dream (of the Antichrist), the web of illusion that man can be his own god, that he can live a full and complete life without recognition of the authority of Jesus Christ."[1]

Satan ultimately didn't triumph when it came to David's temptation, though it must have looked for a while like he had. When you look at the punishment David and all of Israel went through for his sin, it must have looked like Satan had won. But it was really the Lord's punishment. It was the hand of the Lord telling David, "Rely only on me." And David had to listen. While David did listen briefly to Satan's humanistic lie, ultimately David understood Who God was.

The main difference is this: The Man of Sin will never acknowledge God. He will hate God. Prophecy teacher, John Walvoord, writes,

The future ruler was described in an unusual way by Daniel, "He will show no regard for the gods of his fathers or for the one desired by women, nor will he regard any god, but will exalt himself above them all" (Dan. 11:37). On the basis of this verse some have considered this ruler a Jew because of the familiar phrase, "the gods [Elohim] of his fathers." In the KJV, "gods" is translated in the singular "God." The usual expression regarding the God of Israel as the God of their fathers is Yahweh, which is unmistakably the God of Israel. The fact that Daniel used "Elohim" is significant because "Elohim" is used both of the true God and of the false gods and is a general word like the English word God. Further, "Elohim" is a natural plural, and though it was sometimes translated in the singular, referring to heathen gods. The point of the passage is not that he will reject the God of Israel, but he will disregard all deities as indicated in the preceding verse where he considered himself greater than any god. The passage included the fact that he will not regard "the one desired by women" (v37). From the Jewish perspective, the desire of women was to fulfill the promise given to Eve of a coming Redeemer to be born of a woman. Undoubtedly, many Jewish women hoped that one of their sons would fulfill this prophecy. Accordingly, "the one desired by women" is the Messiah of Israel. What this passage accordingly predicted was that he, as a Gentile, will have a total disregard for Scripture and its promise of a coming King of Kings. The Antichrist will not only reject simply the God of Israel but all gods, whether pagan or the true God. In other words, he will be an atheist and will consider himself deity.[2]

The Man of Sin will never beseech the Lord. He will never get over himself. The Man of Sin would rather the earth suffer in great distress than to acknowledge God as God.

While humanism plagues our race with its lie today, the Man of Sin will take it to a whole new level. Watch out for this man! Be aware of the lies funneled to him by Satan himself. If you don't, then you too will deceive yourself into counting on your own resources just as David did.

WAS DAVID'S PUNISHMENT TOO HARSH?

Dear friend, know this: when you go against light, you will pay and often you will pay dearly. While Christ has paid the punishment for our sins and we are assured of salvation, that is no guarantee that while we are on this earth we will not bear the consequences of our sins.

Consider that David had been given a lot of light during

all the years he ran from Saul. The Lord had anointed David and lifted him up to be king of Israel in a miraculous way. David, of all people, knew that God was the One he needed to trust.

David's sin wasn't just a lack of confidence in God, it was a public sin. All the people knew David had done this sin. They then needed to be shown how great God is and that it wasn't their collective might that caused them to be victorious. They had unwillingly participated in David's sin and so needed the reminder about Who was in charge.

Writer Samuel Rutherford said, "Swim through your temptations and troubles. Run to the promises; they are our Lord's branches hanging over the water so that His children may take a grip of them." For a time, David had stopped grabbing hold of God's branches and until he turned his trust back to God, he was hopelessly drowning because of his inability to swim on his own.

Consider for a moment how dependent you are on the Lord. Are you tempted to forget His goodness when things are going well in your life? Do you sometimes forget to grab hold of the Lord's branches as you swim through life's waters? Be aware that as you experience great spiritual victory, Satan is then on the prowl more than ever. He knows victory might blind you to your own pride, making you particularly susceptible to stumbling. If the great David can do it, all of us need to take this lesson to heart. In the midst of great victory, never forget Who gave you that victory.

Prophetic Kingdoms

Elaborate murals, huge statues, and larger-than-life portraits of Saddam Hussein could be seen in the entrances to every town, and in every town square in Iraq. How could any of us forget the footage of Iraqi citizens climbing on the statue in Fridos Square in eastern Baghdad, on April 9, 2003, hitting the head with their shoes, then tying a rope around its neck and attempting to take it down. With help from an American tank, the statue was pulled down as citizens cheered in the streets. After many years of living under the thumb of a cruel dictator, they could finally celebrate.

Why did Saddam erect statues of himself? Pride. Pride of a magnitude few of us could ever comprehend.

Nebuchadnezzar had a dream about another figure we read about in Daniel 2:31-35,

> Thou, O king, sawest, and behold a great image. This great image, whose brightness was excellent, stood before thee; and the form thereof was terrible. This image's head was of fine gold, his breast and his arms of silver, his belly and his thighs of brass, His legs of iron, his feet part of iron and part of clay. Thou sawest till that a stone was cut out without hands, which smote the image upon his feet that were of iron and clay, and brake them to pieces. Then was the iron, the clay, the brass, the silver, and the gold, broken to pieces together, and became like the chaff of the summer threshing floors; and the wind carried them away, that no place was found for them: and the stone that smote the image became a great mountain, and filled the whole earth.

This figure represented future events that would shape the world. In past years some scholars raised questions about whether Daniel was a genuine biblical prophet on the premise that prophecy of future events is impossible. John Walvoord wrote that Porphyry decided that the Book of Daniel was so accurate in describing future events that it must have been written after the fact. He advanced the theory that the book was a forgery, written in the Maccabean period about 175 B.C. His attack on the Book of Daniel aroused immediate opposition and caused Jerome (A.D. 347-420) to write his own commentary on Daniel in which he answered Porphyry in detail. For another 1,300 years Daniel was considered as a genuine book by orthodox Christians and Jews until modern liberalism arose in the seventeenth century.

Critics of the Bible as the inspired Word of God picked

up Porphyry's idea and attempted to prove that Daniel was not a genuine book of the Bible. Many conservative scholars have answered their objections in full. However, the biggest discovery was a copy of Daniel in the Dead Sea Scrolls (c. 100 B.C.); on the basis of premises entertained by the liberals themselves, this proved it was impossible for the book to have been written in the second century B.C. and that it clearly was written many years before. Both Jewish and Christian scholars have attested to the genuine character of the Book of Daniel. The proof includes recognition by Christ Himself of "Daniel the prophet" (Mat. 24:15).[1]

Isn't it amazing that it was this prophecy of the image in Nebuchadnezzar's dream that so disturbed liberal scholars because of its accuracy? Their mouths have been stopped by the discovery of the Dead Sea scrolls which prove that Daniel was written well before any of the events prophesied took place. This is yet more proof that we can trust God's Word. Any honest scholar can look at world history and see how Nebuchadnezzar's dream was fulfilled to the most exact detail. However, when they do this, they will see that the prophecy of the toes is yet to be fulfilled.

It is yet more proof that one of the reasons God put prophecy in the Bible is so that our own faith can be strengthened. We can indeed trust God when He says that after seven years the ten toes made of a mixture of iron and clay come together during the time of tribulation, God will Himself descend with His saints and destroy every work of the Antichrist. He will not only smash humanism into powder but will then fill the entire earth with His presence and glory. It will be much more glorious than the destruction of any statue of Saddam Hussein.

We see great events playing out on the world stage. Democracy is being brought to regions of the world that never before understood the dignity of individual citizens or the joy of liberty. World health organizations are working around the clock to stem the tide of SARS, a disease that might become another black plague. An unprecedented ability to communicate ideas and beliefs to any part of the world and to any person in the world is quickly becoming commonplace. The ability to move produce and goods around the world makes it possible as never before to bring significant relief to regions of the world that suffer. These world-shaping events are literally changing the course of history. They are giving us even more evidence that events of prophecy are being fulfilled before our eyes. These events shouldn't dismay us or discourage us, rather they should add to our faith and cause us to say with the Apostle John, "Even so, come Lord Jesus."

One day everyone, even the Man of Sin, the false prophet, Satan himself, and all the demons will acknowledge God for Who He really is. Philippians 2:10-11 gives us great hope when it says, "That at the name of Jesus every knee should bow, of things in heaven, and things in earth, and things under the earth; And that every tongue should confess that Jesus Christ is Lord, to the glory of God the Father."

Every knee bowing. Every tongue confessing. Imagine the glory of such a moment.

If life ever gets you down and you feel discouraged by the sin, humanism and hardship around you, think of that day. Think of that moment when the stone cut without hands bowls over the earth and shows every man, woman, and child once and for all Who is really in control.

Living in the Present

If this will be true in the future, why do you and I have such a hard time living like it is true in the present? If it is going to happen that every tongue will confess Christ then why do we allow our own tongues to not confess His name to friends and coworkers? If every person will acknowledge Christ's sovereignty, why does the world intimidate us?

It is a lack of perspective. We are not fixing our gaze on the eternal. We are losing our focus and consequently, our power.

Won't you take a minute to pray this prayer?

Lord, I acknowledge that you are the God of the Universe, the Creator of the Heavens and the earth. You are in control and in charge, and there is nothing I can do that can come close to Your power and strength. I pray right now that I will understand just how great You are, that I will get a truer picture of Your power in my own soul so I'm not ashamed to witness for You. Help me to stay aware that one day every tongue will confess your name and that I need to keep living minute by minute as a testimony to Your grace in my life. Give me an understanding of how to live life to show to the world that You are in charge. In Your Name, Amen.

This poem from an unknown author will give you encouragement.

> The world's great heart is aching.
> Aching fiercely in the night.
> And God alone can hear it—
> And God alone give light.
>
> The men to hear the message
> And speak the living Word.
> And you and I, my brother,
> And the missions who have heard.
>
> We grovel among trifles
> And our spirits fret and toss.
> While above us burns the vision
> Of Christ upon the cross.
>
> And the blood of Christ streaming
> From His pierced hands and side.
> And the lips of Christ as saying
> Tell the lost that I have died.
>
> No power of man shall thwart us
> No strongholds shall dismay.

When God commands obedience
And love has led the way.

God is in charge. It's up to us as believers to show that
to the world.

CHAPTER 6

The Unholy Trinity

Jordan River
Matthew 3:17-4:11

THE THREE STOOD AS ONE. The Father's voice resounded over the throng, the fluttering dove wings represented the Spirit, while the radiant Son stood, still in the River Jordan, beside John the Baptist.

The Trinity personified for all to see. A living statement that this was no ordinary man.

Jesus stepped out of the water, the moment over—but not really. People flocked around Him. Children rushed to sit in His lap. He looked kind, gentle, calm.

Satan observed from a distance, whatever was left of his heart growing cold within him.

The ministry was beginning. He had tried to murder Him as a baby, but now here He was, looking stronger than ever.

Satan hated not knowing everything. Who could have believed that the Creator would send His own Son to be born as one of them? Sent to a poor family, of all things. Jesus had seemed content for the last thirty years, to grow, learn, and work with Joseph. Satan didn't know Jesus' purpose, but he sensed that things were changing. This viewing of three as one had never happened quite this obviously before. There had been much in Scripture indicating this would happen, yet, even Satan felt like he wasn't prepared to view the Son of God in the flesh.

This was the beginning and Satan wasn't sure exactly what it was the beginning of . . . but he knew something was happening, something unusual loomed on the horizon, something opposed to Satan's every wish.

Someday he would bring his own son to the fore; he would jump out of obscurity and take the world by storm. His handsome face would turn the hearts of all who knew him and when he spoke, the entire world would listen.

They couldn't help it.

No one could.

But the glory of this moment. Satan couldn't deny it had its own unique feeling, a different emotion than he had ever felt before. Satan turned his face away. He couldn't look at Jesus, not right now. Jesus looked as He had when He stood beside the Father that fateful moment he himself had chosen to go against all he knew.

Satan blinked. In some ways, Jesus blended in so well that it didn't seem like this man could be the Creator of the universe. Somehow though, that very blending in, that identification with mankind, set him apart.

Satan watched as Jesus talked to John. What a contrast those two men presented. John with his camel hair coat, Jesus in simple garb. Satan could only hope that people would continue to be as obtuse as they had ever been, that they would miss the signs. The wonders. The miracle of His birth. The shepherds, the kings, the adoration. Most people wouldn't understand it. Satan had been around long enough to know that unless people sought truth, they never would find it.

Satan trembled. It was time for the battle of his life. If Jesus really was a man, then He could be tempted with evil. Satan had planned this temptation for many years now, ever since Jesus had returned from Egypt. The temptation had to be perfect and ready—definitely after this moment, Jesus could be tempted. Surely He had felt great reassurance when the Father and the Spirit confirmed before all of Israel that He was the Son of God. If a moment ever existed when His heart could be tempted with pride, it had to be now.

Satan thought through Scripture passages, remembering

the ones he intended to use. He would use His own words against the One who wrote them. He laughed within himself. The irony of it all. Eve and David had only needed a push in the right direction, but he knew it would take more than that this time.

Jesus was at one of His highest points, and this was the time to strike. The lush grass around the river looked inviting, but Satan looked to the barren hills in the distance. A much better place. Jesus was a man after all. He must reach the limitations of His manhood before He would be ready for the first temptation.

Everything was falling into place.

Jesus would collapse. Maybe Jesus was his man.

* *

IMAGINE YOURSELF IN THE WILDERNESS, NOT HAVING EATEN FOR FORTY DAYS, BEING TEMPTED TO MAKE BREAD FROM A STONE. If we had that power, not much would stop us from gratifying our flesh. Yet, we see Jesus resisting the devil three times, even completing the Scriptures shot at Him. What a wonderful example Jesus is for us as we study Satan's tricks and temptations. Of all the Biblical characters we've studied so far, only Christ didn't succumb.

Satan's temptation of Christ was no small thing. Satan used every ounce of his power to cause Christ to fall. How it must have grated on him to watch our Lord consistently resist him and even order him to be gone. Look at Matthew 4:10-11, "Then saith Jesus unto him, Get thee hence, Satan: for it is written, Thou shalt worship the Lord thy God, and him only shalt thou serve. Then the devil leaveth him, and, behold, angels came and ministered unto him."

I have often wondered what the angels talked about to the Lord as they ministered to Him. Did they comfort Him and give Him strength for the next phase of His ministry? We know they fed him and ministered to his physical needs while the Devil was off licking his wounds, plotting his next hurtful work.

Jesus refused to be Satan's man.

Jesus would go on to defeat Satan forever.

Satan had to know, even then, his days were numbered.

KEY TO OVERCOMING TEMPTATION

Do you see a pattern to Satan's temptations? In both David and Jesus, we see that Satan struck just after a great victory. Jesus had just been baptized by John the Baptist. At the moment of His baptism, the Father spoke words of love and affirmation to the world while the Spirit showed Himself in the form of a dove.

Satan tempted Christ as though He were a mere man and could be tempted as we can be. Christ responded to the temptation as we should in the power of the Spirit and with the Word of God. Are you beginning to understand a great spiritual truth? Watch out after a victory! The devil is lying in wait, wanting to use our own propensity for pride to his own advantage. This can happen to all of us whether we are new Christians or we've known the Lord for many years.

Thirty-five-year-old Sarah has faithfully served the Lord for many years. When her bid was accepted to buy a starter home, she was elated. Although she had hoped to be married by this time in her life, she was glad the Lord had blessed her financially. The next day, Sarah's coworker, Stan, asked her for a date. Normally, Sarah would have been ready to say no to such a request. She had already taken the Scripture's warning against being unequally yoked with unbelievers to heart. She knew Stan wasn't a Christian and so had already determined that they couldn't date. Yet, her guard was down because of her victory the day before and she agreed to go out with Stan. Several months later, Sarah had to break off her relationship with Stan. She saw then that she should have been more on guard after her victory. She understood she could have avoided a lot of trouble if she had just said no to the temptation in the first place.

Determine right now to be extra careful after a victory

in your life. Realize that the Devil knows your guard might be down at that moment and so will bring a temptation into your life that you might not be able to resist. Maybe you have been tempted to browse sinful sites on the Internet. Perhaps you are tempted toward feeling prideful because of your previous faithful service to the Lord. It could be that you have been tempted to drop off in your church attendance. Whatever the case, why don't you take a moment and ask God for special strength for the kind of temptation you are facing? He has promised to help you. He understands your exact need. Remember that in all points He was tempted as we are (Hebrews 4:15), and He knows the exact help to give you so you can overcome even the toughest enticement.

I encourage you to not let Satan use a spiritual victory to his advantage. Be on the lookout and make sure that you don't become a tool in Satan's hand.

THE UNHOLY TRINITY

Just as we see the Holy Trinity depicted during Christ's baptism, so we see how Satan, the Great Duplicator, desires to have his own trinity. Of course, it won't be a holy trinity but rather an unholy trinity. This union will consist of Satan, the Antichrist, and the False Prophet, with Satan, of course, giving power to the other two.

Satan loves to counterfeit God. He enjoys seeing how close to the truth he can make a lie look. Why does he do this? He wants to deceive as many people as possible. If something he does has at least a few earmarks of truth, people will be more ready to receive it.

What is the unholy trinity? We have Satan depicted in the verses we read previously (Rev. 11:13-14) as the Dragon. In comparing him to the Holy Trinity, he would be the father. That name fits him when we understand that God calls him the "father of lies" in John 8:44. The Antichrist could be compared as the exact opposite of the Son of God. And the False Prophet, who will work signs and wonders that bring glory to the Antichrist, is the exact opposite of the gentle

Holy Spirit.

The Dragon. The Antichrist. The False Prophet. An unholy alliance that will dupe the world.

For a brief moment it will look like Satan has won.

But Satan has already lost.

Satan is a loser.

He lost a long time ago. Dear friend, never lose sight of this truth. This will help you as you live your Christian life. Understand that the last chapter has already been written, and Satan—even as he continues to try to thwart God's plans—is only bringing God's predictions to pass.

This motivates me when I am tempted to feel discouraged in this sin-sick world, and I believe if you take this truth to heart, it will help you to view life through the blood of the Lamb. You are a conqueror through Him that loved you. If you never forget this, spiritual victory is yours for the taking.

THE EVIL PARODY

Read Revelation 13:11 one more time: "And I beheld another beast coming up out of the earth; and he had two horns like a lamb, and he spake as a dragon."

Writer Edgar James explains that "'in that he speaks as a dragon' means that Satan, the dragon, gives him his authority and empowers him. The False Prophet, like the Antichrist, will be working the works of Satan."[1]

The late commentator M.R. De Haan explains,

In an evil parody of the Holy Spirit, who glorifies Christ (John 16:14), this third personage (the false prophet) seeks to cause men to worship the beast (the Antichrist), who has received his authority from the dragon (Satan). He is three times in Revelation called "the false prophet" and is directly associated with the beast and the dragon (Rev. 16:13; 19:20; 20:10). John sees another (that is, "another of the same type") beast (Greek therion, "dangerous beast") arising from the earth, instead of from the sea like the first beast. Since the first beast is a man, so is the second, but their backgrounds are different. There has been much speculation as to the identity of this second beast. Since he is later called the false prophet, he apparently first comes to world attention as a miracle-working religious leader, professing to convey supernaturally inspired messages to mankind. His "prophecies" of course, are not from God but from Satan, though it may well be that he will first become known (possibly before the tribulation) as a man supposedly receiving messages from God. He professes to be a true prophet but is in reality a false prophet.[2]

De Haan's observations are dead on. They make perfect sense especially in today's era of "signs and wonders" Christianity. I don't believe that these signs and wonders of faith healers are biblical. Rather, I believe they are preparing the world to receive another sort of man, a man who purports to be from God but is really receiving messages directly from Satan. A man will fool the world mainly because he can perform "miracles" for all to see.

The unholy trinity will hoodwink the world, and the Son of Satan's ability to use quasi-Christian terminology (like the idea of the trinity) will make it palatable for the masses.

Most children dislike taking medicine. I noticed at the drug store the other day an advertisement offering over twenty-one flavors that would disguise the taste of the required medicine. Such an addition would surely make the medicine easier to swallow and in the same way, Satan's use of Christianese will camouflage the dangerous new age properties of his falsehoods. A new religion for a new age. The Old Lie will seem fresh and inviting. Many people will willingly open their mouths and take this poison-laced "medicine."

NEW ATHEISM

There are many who might think atheism is Satan's ultimate triumph. All those years when the Iron Curtain was still a reality, there were many Christians who thought the Devil had totally conquered those nations. While I'm sure Satan is happy when people believe there isn't a God, he would rather people believe he is the true god. Satan knows that if people begin to see all false religions as leading to an ultimate glory, then he has triumphed. During Communist rule, the anti-god teaching was confined mainly to Communist countries. This doesn't mean there weren't atheists in other countries, but the teaching stayed somewhat confined because of the political inability of the nations. The Iron Curtain kept not only capitalism and commerce from reaching inside; it kept its people chained to its anti-religion, unable to accept any other teaching.

The same principle has been true of the Islamic countries. Though I understand that Satan is pleased with any false religion, his real goal is to spread his falsehood to the world. Islamic teaching is too exclusive for the Devil's liking. Like the Iron Curtain, it keeps its adherents from accepting any new teaching. And certainly that kind of "exclusivity" would keep the Arab nations from accepting the Antichrist whom we know from Scriptures unites the world and makes peace with the Jews and Israel.

Now, we see the events since America's September 11, 2001, and the change in Saddam Hussein's regime in Iraq as a real change not only in the world's perception of Islam, but also as a change which I believe will happen more and more: the Muslims themselves becoming more accepting of other philosophies and religions. If in the next years the Arab people start to categorize Islamic teaching into what they believe and what they reject, they will start to adopt a more "democratic" way of thinking.

I don't believe democracy is inherently evil. I certainly love living in America more than I would any place else, however it is easy to see that a democratic way of thinking will help usher in Satan's world-uniting religion.

Dave Hunt was one of the few prophecy scholars who predicted this about Islam. He also thought the same thing of Communism. He writes in his book, *Global Peace and the Rise of the Antichrist*,

> The collapse of Communism in Eastern Europe and the introduction of "freedom of religion" is not a setback for Satan. Atheism is not the ultimate triumph that Satan seeks, but to persuade mankind to believe in false gods, and eventually in the "God-power" within. Those who think they have been liberated to fulfill their own desires are blind to the fact that they have subtly become the slaves of the Enemy of their souls and are doing his will. Satan transforms himself "into an angel of light" and inspires his emissaries to masquerade as "the ministers of righteousness" (2 Cor. 11:14,15). He is the father of "positive thinking," and is a master at "how to win friends and influence people." He prevents his false theology from being unmasked by accusing those who attempt to expose it of being "negative" and "divisive."[3]

Hunt mentions earlier in the same book:

> Is it mere coincidence that both religious and political unity are coming together at this moment? The time is ripe. Even Iraq's naked aggression in taking over Kuwait in August 1990 became the basis for giving the world new hope for an end to military conflict. As Marlin Fitzwater, former White House spokesman declared, "The process of war is forging a new blueprint for world peace."

> Saddam Hussein's call for a Holy War (Jihad) not only weakened Arab solidarity but raised questions about the very concept of Jihad. Such questions when pondered in the days ahead could lead Muslims

to begin to see themselves not as a separate world at odds with everyone else but as a part of a religiously pluralistic international community that is learning to live and respect and cooperate together.[4]

President George H.W. Bush, George W's father, said after the Gulf War that we were entering a "new world order." I stood in my pulpit even then and said I thought it was really a new world disorder, and so it is. Satan's plan is surely coming to pass as he continues to forge together formerly "exclusive" terminologies and religions into what he thinks will be a seamless whole. The real truth is, order will give way to disorder greater than any the world has witnessed before. The world will never be united until it unites under Jesus Christ.

There will be no peace until the Prince of Peace comes. But brace yourself, you will hear a lot of talk about "peace" before it's all over.

"TRUTH-FILLED" LIES

The real secret behind the Antichrist will be his ability to tell blatant lies that not only will the world believe, but that he will believe himself. His ability to lie will surpass even Mohammed Saeed Al-Sahhaf, Iraq's former minister of information. He was no stranger to the media and its impact—and to Iraq's rough politics. He was studying to be an English teacher when he got his start in politics in 1963 by joining a violent group led by Saddam that targeted opponents of the Baath party.

After a 1963 coup, he revealed the whereabouts of his brother-in-law, an army general and the country's military prosecutor, who was then killed by Baath party militias. By handing over his relative, this man proved his loyalty to the Baath party.

A Baathist regime was overthrown in another coup the same year, but the party came back five years later. Al-Sahhaf was put in charge of securing the radio and television stations and then put at the helm of both. He was known for his temper—even kicking TV and radio employees who displeased him.

Al-Sahhaf, who is in his early 60s, became information minister in 2001. Before that, he was foreign minister, from 1993 to 2001. He also has served as Iraq's ambassador to India, Italy and the United Nations.

Early in the 2003 conflict, television pictures of U.S. tanks in Baghdad seemed undeniable, but Iraqi President Saddam Hussein's spokesman denied them anyway, with his usual flair for insult.

"There is no presence of American infidels in the city of Baghdad," Al-Sahhaf asserted outside Baghdad's Palestine Hotel on Monday. A day later, when the hotel came under U.S. tank fire, the Iraqi information minister had to admit to journalists staying there that coalition forces were in the capital. But, smiling, he made it sound like it was all part of Iraq's plan: "We blocked them inside the city. Their rear is blocked," he said in hurried remarks that were a departure from his daily news conference. After being shown footage of Iraqi soldiers surrendering: Al-Sahhaf said, "Those are not Iraqi soldiers at all."

According to one newspaper article, some Arab commentators have dubbed Al-Sahhaf the "Iraqi Goebbels," after Joseph Goebbels, Hitler's master propagandist. [5]

The scary truth is that the Antichrist will be able to convince the world of an even greater lie than the one Al-Sahhaf tried to perpetuate. The lie will deceive many, and only a few will escape.

However, there will be some who challenge the beast. There will be a remnant saved through the 144,000 Jewish evangelists who overcome the beast. Look at Revelation 12:11, "And they overcame him by the blood of the Lamb, and by the word of their testimony; and they loved not their lives unto the death."

My friend, Pastor Erwin Lutzer, wrote about this:

And how does this believing remnant counteract the attack of Satan? Just as we [believers] do. First, they overcame him by the blood of the Lamb. Satan can no longer accuse those who have been acquitted by God, thanks to the sacrifice of Christ. Every just accusation is now silenced. As we read in Revelation 1:5, "And from Jesus Christ, who is the faithful witness, and the first begotten of the dead, and the prince of the kings of the earth. Unto him that loved us, and washed us from our sins in his own blood." No matter how extensive Satan's end-time network, the power of the Cross still stands. Indeed, the power of the Cross is seen most clearly when the forces of evil seem to triumph.[6]

Dear friend, remember the power of the Cross as you go about your daily business. Remember that Jesus Christ has more power than Satan could ever dream of possessing. Don't underestimate the power that is within you or the fact that you can overcome Satan though the blood of the Lamb.

Why don't you take a minute to pray this prayer?

Lord, thank you for defeating Satan at the cross. Help me to be alert to temptation and continue to abide in Your power. Please give me the strength to look to the future with confidence, knowing that You are ultimately in control. Help me to use this knowledge of the end times as a catalyst in my witnessing to others.

CHAPTER 7

The False Sacrifice

Galilee, Israel
Matthew 8

THE DEMONS DIDN'T WANT TO HEAR HIS NAME EVER AGAIN. They gathered at the tombs. They howled and screamed for their misery, for their master and to irritate their hosts, John of Galilee and David. Although they had been possessed by legions of demons for years, they still didn't know what to do when the demons howled like this. The men put their hands over their ears and huddled together.

"Convenient bodies," the demon thought, "these two are unable to fight us."

"Jesus is here to destroy us," shouted one of his cohorts, "I know He is."

"Stop! Do not say His name!" The demon ordered.

"We cannot help it. The very rocks cry out."

"That's why we should not say it."

"I thought our own prince was working on Him," another devil offered.

"He is, and soon he will prevail."

A hush fell for a moment over the throng of spirits. The demon heard John speak.

"We must go find this man."

"Who?" David scratched his nose.

"Jesus."

The howls started again.

John beat his chest with his fists, "We must rid ourselves of these miserable demons."

David put his head in his hands, "Yes, we must. They give us no peace, day or night."

"There is no rest for the wicked," a demon shouted while the other demons took up the chant. John and David crossed their arms and waited.

The demon knew that if he kept everyone howling, John and David wouldn't talk any more. The humans had been possessed for so long, they knew to give up once the noise started.

We can't howl forever, he thought. He could only hope the men would fall asleep in spite of the noise. Then he and his friends could have a brief rest before starting again.

But the men stayed awake.

He tried calling on other demons beyond the many gathered. These mortals were usually so compliant but today they seemed determined to wait them out.

He didn't know if they could overcome the men this time. They had resumed talking about Jesus and seemed oblivious to the howls and groans around them.

They stood.

He panicked. "I should have called in Lucifer before this!" He wished he was wrong about what they were going to do.

"We must go now," John said. David started walking.

He ordered the demons to keep screaming, to keep moving, to try to stop the men from walking.

But, for once, they couldn't stop them.

The two men kept walking, sure of where to go.

The demon could sense they were getting closer to Him. His spirit body recoiled. He didn't want to continue, but he had no choice.

The two men walked all night. Now the early rays of dawn bathed the grassy field before them. And there was the Sea. Stately in its beauty. He shuddered. He hated the Sea of Galilee.

And there He was. Standing there. Staring right through them. He shouted with every ounce of strength. "What have you to do with us, Jesus of Nazareth?" He spoke what all of them had thought all the night before, "Are you come to torment us before our time?"

Sudden screams filled the air. They were out of the men. They were traveling not of their own volition. All of them. Into the unknown. Tortured perhaps forever without a body.

No body. No more horrible fate could be contemplated.

He spoke quickly, hoping he could be heard above the screams, "Let us go into those swine! We beg of you!"

He was inside the pigs almost. Just before he left, he noticed the men falling to the ground. The pigs ran down the slope and into the water.

He knew one day he would stand in judgment. Perhaps the swine were the beginning of that day.

* *

JUDGMENT. The day the Son of Satan declares himself to be God will be the day the Jewish people begin to understand that their own judgment has begun. They will look in horror, seeing their worst nightmare.

Rebuilding their Temple was a dream come true. It was their final triumph—the culmination of years of struggle to maintain their homeland.

And when the Antichrist demands worship, they will see just how badly they had been deceived.

One day on the shores of the Sea of Galilee, Jesus showed his power over the demons by casting a legion of them into a herd of pigs. One day, the Antichrist will retaliate setting himself up as God.

The false sacrifice.

The world didn't accept the sacrifice of the spotless Lamb of God on the cross. Instead they must gaze at the false one.

THE OTHER SIDE OF JUDGMENT

Along with this judgment comes mercy. Even as the people

react in horror to the sacrifice, those who know Scripture will know what they need to do next.

The false Messiah will force the Jews to flee to Petra, their only hope of safety.

Do you see, dear Christian, how merciful God is in all of this?

God could have simply destroyed this earth in the last day without making one prediction about how that would come about. He didn't have to give signs and prophecies. But He gives the world signs and prophecies as a warning.

Look at Jesus' words in Mark 13:14-20,

> But when ye shall see the abomination of desolation, spoken of by Daniel the prophet, standing where it ought not, (let him that readeth understand,) then let them that be in Judaea flee to the mountains: And let him that is on the housetop not go down into the house, neither enter therein, to take any thing out of his house: And let him that is in the field not turn back again for to take up his garment. But woe to them that are with child, and to them that give suck in those days! And pray ye that your flight be not in the winter. For in those days shall be affliction, such as was not from the beginning of the creation which God created unto this time, neither shall be. And except that the Lord had shortened those days, no flesh should be saved: but for the elect's sake, whom he hath chosen, he hath shortened the days.

Jesus is saying to the Jewish people that the abomination of desolation is the clear sign to flee to the mountains. Our merciful God delivers judgment even as He offers compassion.

Several months ago, I started to feel a slight ache in the back of my neck as I walked my normal 3½-mile walk. The pain didn't spread anywhere else, so I didn't think it could be related to my heart. I thought possibly I had pulled a muscle or something minor like that. It wasn't until several weeks later that I started having the pain when I was at rest, and this time the pain traveled down my arms and chest. After a series of tests, they learned that my arteries were almost 90 percent blocked, and I underwent five-way bypass surgery. Praise God it was successful, and today I have to honestly say I've never felt better.

I was one of the fortunate ones. I felt pain. Many people who suffer from heart problems don't know it until they have their first heart attack. God was merciful because He gave me pain.

In the same way, God is merciful to the world even as it experiences the pain of his judgment. Tim LaHaye writes,

> Even when God decides that the time for judgment has come, He doesn't unload all His wrath at once. Even in judgment, He shows mercy. His goal is never to inflict as much suffering as possible, but as little. Therefore, the Lord normally employs escalating judgments in order to get our attention and persuade us to change our life course. He increases the intensity of His discipline in proportion to the stubbornness of our hearts [I'm inserting here: in proportion to those unsaved people during the Tribulation period]. He takes no pleasure in causing us distress, but He takes less pleasure in allowing us to walk blindly into oblivion.[1]

Those who criticize a literal interpretation of the Word of God and prophecy say that we believe in a God Who will punish the world with the terrible events of the Tribulation; and since He is going to do it anyway, it doesn't matter about the rest of the human race who doesn't know the Lord. Our God will visit His wrath upon the earth. The crazy logic continues that then we can just sit back and twiddle our thumbs because we are going up in the Rapture.

Nothing could be further from the truth. Even while He is sending His wrath, He is showing His mercy by predicting specific events that people will have to recognize. Pain brings awareness of other problems. On the other side of judgment is mercy.

Dear friend, why don't you take a moment right now and thank God for that mercy?

THE SARS PLAGUE

Of all the headlines screaming at us today, the outbreak of the SARS virus had to be one of the scariest. As I read and studied about how this virus began and how it spread, I couldn't help but see a correlation between this and the plagues God will send on the world during the Great Tribulation. And I also thought about God's mercy in that this virus hasn't yet taken on epidemic proportions for it is surely close to such a point.

SARS' overall death rate of about 6 percent is far lower than that of AIDS, ebola or malaria; but if enough people catch the illness, even a low rate could be a catastrophe. The Spanish flu epidemic of 1918-19 had a death rate of less than 3 percent, but so many people became infected that it killed more than 20 million people in just eighteen months. According to a *Time* article by Michael D. Lemonick and Alice Park, the financial fallout during the worst part of the SARS outbreak was catastrophic. The deadly respiratory illness may have started in a rural province of China, but its impact—economic and otherwise—is rippling around the world, spreading even faster than the virus that caused it. North American airline bookings to Hong Kong plunged more than 85 percent. In the first two weeks of April 2003, visitor arrivals to Singapore dropped 61 percent. From February to March, hotel business in Asia plummeted 25 percent. Hong Kong carrier Cathay Pacific cut its weekly flights 45 percent, and during the worst of the crisis, the virus cost Canada $30 million a day. Even the Catholic Church of Singapore suspended confessions in booths and granted "general forgiveness" to believers. In Ontario, worshippers were asked to refrain from kissing icons, dipping their hands in holy water or sharing communion wine.[2]

The real worry about SARS is the variations the virus seems capable of producing. The disease doesn't seem to strike a certain demographic; its victims vary from the typical people with compromised immune systems to young people in excellent health. Even its transmission seems to be a mystery. While some people got the virus from other people who had it, 300 people in one apartment complex in Hong Kong came down with SARS even though many of them seemed to have no direct contact with one another.

Just one epidemic like this tells us how precarious the world's financial and health systems really are. It wouldn't take much for this world's house of cards to come tumbling down; in fact the Bible predicts this in chilling detail during the Great Tribulation.

Faith for the Present

Now, while we see signs of coming judgment on the horizon, we still walk by faith. The disciple Thomas refused to believe that Jesus had been raised from the dead until he could see Him with his own eyes. After seeing him, "Jesus saith unto him, Thomas, because thou hast seen me, thou hast believed: blessed are they that have not seen, and yet have believed" (John 20:29). Yes, it requires faith to believe in Jesus Christ, but it is not blind faith.

I remember one of my university friends saying to me, "If God would just open up the Heavens and show me everything in Heaven and show me Himself, then I would believe." His arrogance astounded me even then. I knew how precise the Bible has proven itself to be. We had the accuracy of the Bible proved by the finding of the Dead Sea Scrolls. We knew the Jews had returned to the land as a direct fulfillment of Bible prophecy. And he wanted to see the Heavens opened up.

I am sad to say that my friend never did trust Christ. And one day he may see the Heavens open up. But what he sees will scare him to death. Plagues, terrible tornadoes, huge locusts, death.

It won't be a pretty sight.

While there has never been an excuse for unbelief, there will surely be no excuse then. But even in the midst of that terrible time, God will show His mercy by the fact that He gives the earth seven more years to believe.

After that time, there won't be a second chance.

Ready to Rebuild

Let's go back to an earlier thought in this chapter. When Jesus commanded the demons to enter the swine, we see a chilling foreshadow of the terrible day when the Antichrist sacrifices a pig on the altar. But remember this, for the Antichrist to sacrifice a pig, there must be a temple in which to perform that sacrifice. Some of the most exciting developments concerning Bible prophecy concern the Jews' preparation to rebuild their temple. This is beyond any believer's wildest dreams.

Years ago, it was exciting enough to watch Israel coming back on the scene and become the center of the world's news; now with the temple preparations, I feel so privileged to be part of a time when so much evidence of the Lord's coming is unfolding before us.

Many years ago, my good friend Jimmy DeYoung of Shofar Communications told me about Solomon's attempt to lay the cornerstone of the future Jewish temple. I recently interviewed Gershon Solomon about his work with the Temple Mount Faithful.

Q: On August 20, 2003, the government of Israel reopened the Temple Mount to Israelis, Jews, Christians and non-Muslim's. How did this make you feel?

A: The opening of the Temple Mount by the Israeli government was an important decision. For three years the Temple Mount was closed to Jews, Christians and other non-Muslims after Ariel Sharon went up onto the Temple Mount. The Temple Mount and Land of Israel Faithful Movement made a number of petitions to the Israeli Supreme Court and held demonstrations calling on the Israeli government to no longer give in to the terrorist threats and to immediately re-open the Temple Mount. The last petition was submitted on August 5, 2003 prior to Tisha b'Av. The Supreme Court asked the Minister of Internal Security, Tsachi Hanegbi, to explain why the Temple Mount had been closed for so long a time and why he was not doing anything to open it. During the discussion of the petition, the judges showed their support of our position. Under pressure from the Supreme Court and our petitions and demonstrations, the Minister stated before the Court that the Temple Mount would be opened immediately after Tisha b'Av which he did on August 20th.

As to how I felt, this was an important decision but, at the same time I felt that it was a terrible mistake to close the Temple Mount in the first place in the face of Arab threats of riots.

At the same time, the opening of the Temple Mount was done under shameful limitations — Jews and Christians are still not allowed to worship on the Temple Mount; Jews are not allowed to pray on the Temple Mount, nor to wear a tallit (prayer shawl) when they go up to the Temple Mount, nor to carry a prayer book, Torah Scroll or any other Jewish symbols or items. The First Temple was built three thousand years ago by the Jews and their king, King Solomon, c.1000 BCE and the Second Temple was built in 516 BCE. The Arabs occupied the land of Israel, Jerusalem, and the Temple Mount in 638 BCE, and robbed the Jews of the holy hill, which the Jews had dedicated and glorified for the Beloved God of Israel, and built two buildings of foreign pagan worship as a result of an imperialistic occupation.

The opening of the Temple Mount, especially with such shameful limitations, is not enough. It is not what the God of Israel expects His people to do in these end-times in which we are now living. They do not allow me to go up, despite the fact that the holy campaign of me and my friends from the Faithful Movement is admired by them and so often that we are even their own messengers exactly as Ariel Sharon, before becoming Prime Minister, stated in meetings that he had with me. But I must immediately say that they can never stop my spirit from being on the holy hill of God in the place which is the heart, soul and eternal focus of my people. The Arabs have stated that they do not want me to walk on the Temple Mount because, in their eyes, I am the symbol of the Jewish struggle to re-liberate the Temple Mount and to rebuild the house of God.

I was called by God as a great privilege, and my life and the lives of my friends from the Faithful Movement are completely dedicated to this end. We act day and night with great devotion to bring it about in our lifetime as God expects of us and His people to do. This has been the dream and the desire of the Jewish people for almost 2000 years since the destruction of the Second Temple, and it symbolizes everything in their desire to be redeemed nationally and spiritually, to be regathered to the land of Israel which God gave them in an eternal covenant and to rebuild the kingdom of God in the Promised Land, Jerusalem, the Temple Mount and from here, all over the world. Now is God's timing and, as He told us thousands of years ago through His prophets, this great dream, vision and desire should come to pass at this time and at no other time. The Almighty God of Israel told us this in such an exciting and beautiful way throughout His Word in the Tanach and in a very unique and special way in Isaiah 2:1-5,

> The word that Isaiah the son of Amoz saw concerning Judah and Jerusalem. And it shall come to pass in the last days, that the mountain of the Lord's house shall be established on the top of the mountains, and shall be exalted above the hills; and all nations shall flow to it. And many people shall go and say, Come, and let us go up to the mountain of the Lord, to the house of the God of Jacob; and he will teach us of his ways, and we will walk in his paths; for from Zion shall go forth the law, and the word of the Lord from Jerusalem. And he shall judge among the nations,

and shall decide for many people; and they shall beat their swords into plowshares, and their spears into pruning hooks; nation shall not lift up sword against nation, nor shall they learn war any more. O house of Jacob, come, and let us walk in the light of the Lord.

Q: How long has the Temple Mount Faithful Movement been in existence?

A: The Temple Mount Faithful Movement was founded immediately after the Six-Day War of 1967. It was after God gave me the privilege of being together with my unit on the Temple Mount in front of the location of the Holy of Holies, which is today covered by the Dome of the Rock, on the day of the liberation of the Temple Mount by the Israeli forces. The Israeli flag flew from the top of the Dome of the Rock and we stood there with tears of excitement in our eyes and feeling the tremendous significance of this great godly moment, the biggest in the history of Israel. Not too long before that, when I led my unit as a young Israeli officer in the Israeli army of God in a battle in the Golan Heights, I had been severely wounded and God saved my life and spoke to my heart that He had done so for a mission. Then again in 1967 when I stood in front of the God of Israel in His Holy of Holies, I could again hear the voice of the God of Israel speaking to my heart—for this purpose, for the rebuilding of My holy house, I gave your life back to you and anointed you to do it for the rest of your life. I know that this was the call of the God of Israel to all His people, Israel. At the same moment I answered this exciting call and decided to dedicate all my life for this purpose and mission. I thank God that He sent me to fulfill this, the biggest godly end-time mission. In my prayers I continually thank Him for this, the greatest privilege ever.

With the understanding of the significance of this great moment of the return to the Temple Mount, the understanding that a new stage in the end-time redemptional history of

Israel had started, brought about my decision to found The Temple Mount and Land of Israel Faithful Movement, the end-time vessel of God to fulfill all His prophetic plans with Israel and all mankind and to start the campaign and struggle to correct this decision of Moshe Dayan and the Israeli leadership, to re-liberate the Temple Mount, to purify it and to rebuild the Third Temple on it in the same location as that of the First and Second Temples as God commanded us, not as a vision for the distant future, but as a reality and a practical fulfillment and act in the life of our generation as God expects of us. So on the next day I called on fifteen faithful Israelis to the God of Israel and people of Israel and in a historical meeting in Jerusalem with the help of the God of Israel and, thanks to Him, I founded the Temple Mount Faithful Movement.

Q: How can the Temple be built on the Temple Mount when another temple exists on the holy site?

A: There is no doubt that the mosque and Dome of the Rock which exist on the holy site today must first be removed and then the holy site must be purified according to the Jewish biblical godly Law. Then the temple and its complex will be rebuilt on the same location as that of the First and Second Temples, the location which God showed King David. This is a godly law and cannot be changed by even one inch here or there. The Holy of Holies is today covered by the Dome of the Rock and important research shows that the Dome was built at the end of the Seventh Century by a Muslim leader who ruled from Damascus and who had Jewish beliefs. He wanted to build this building to be a house of prayer for the Jews. (You can find an article on this subject on our web site in our latest magazine.) However, this building must also be removed and the Third Temple, like the others, rebuilt by the Jews and not by any foreigner.

Q: Would you comment on what is going to happen in the near future?

A: The near future in Israel and then all over the world will be very exciting and critical. The major part of it will be the rebuilding of the Temple and the coming of Mashiach ben David. Israel will find herself ready to fulfill her godly eternal task, for which God created the Israeli nation to be a holy nation, a kingdom of priests and a treasure among the nations. For this purpose God called Abraham and made the eternal covenant with him and his seed, Israel. For this purpose God regathered the Jewish people to the land that He promised to them where their forefathers lived and built the kingdom of God. For this purpose God recreated the State of Israel in 1948 and brought them back to the Temple Mount, biblical Jerusalem, Judaea, Samaria, Gaza and the Golan Heights.

The prophecy of Ezekiel 36 and 37 speaks of the united tribes of Ephraim and Judah which will become one stick over whom God will place King David. The Mashiach of Israel will become an exciting reality in the near future. We shall also experience the end-time war of all the nations against Israel as prophesied in the Tanach, mainly in Ezekiel 38,39, and Zechariah 12,14. God will show Israel His great miracles when He defeats the nations and, according to the prophet Joel, He will judge them all in the Valley of Jehoshaphat including for the terrible time when they persecuted the people of Israel. [Obadiah] In this war, God will show His beloved people in a time of crisis of leadership in Israel, that He is the only leader of His people and, as He said in Ezekiel, they will forever know that He is their only God and Father and they are His beloved people. After this war all the nations will accept, worship and love only the One Living God of Israel, the God of Abraham, Isaac and Jacob. The kingdom of God, the focus of which will be the Temple Mount in Jerusalem, will cover all the earth. The time until this great day will be a very critical time of troubles which actually have already started in Israel and even all over the world. Israel is in the midst of attack, terror, hatred, anti-Semitism and rejection by most of the nations and the UN and the European Union. This will be a time of birth pains of the redemption of Israel and then, through Israel, of all the world. This time, which is a time of judgment, was depicted by Joel as a very difficult and terrible time but also a time of the saving and redemption of Israel.

Q: Would you encourage people to come to Israel to see for themselves what God is doing there?

A: Sure! I encourage, and even more I call on, everyone in the world to come to Israel with a clean heart of love for the God of Israel, His holy mountain, Yerushalaim and the land of Israel and His people to show their encouragement and standing with the people of Israel which is so needed at this critical time more than at any time in the past. It is no accident that God told all the nations to love Him through His people, Israel. They should come and encourage the Israeli people to immediately rebuild the Temple as the key godly event for all the events that will follow. They should encourage The Temple Mount and Land of Israel Faithful Movement, the end-time vessel of God, which is so busy and acting intensively at this critical time to bring about all this godly prophetic vision and make it a reality in our lifetime. Like Israel which has an eternal godly mission and task and cannot run away from her destiny, all the nations cannot run away from their task and destiny which has as its focus in the near future, Yerushalaim, the Temple Mount and the rebuilt eternal Temple. The biblical message of the God of Israel to His people, Israel—Trust in God—should be, and will be in the near future, the foundation for all mankind.

I am so glad Gershon Solomon took the time to answer my questions concerning the Jewish temple.

Another Jewish author, Lambert Dolphin, wrote some information regarding the beginning of the current temple movement. He has graciously given me permission to quote part of his article, "Moving Toward a Third Jewish Temple":

In the summer of 1983 Rabbi Yehuda Getz, the former Rabbi of the Western Wall (he died in 1995), broke through the Western Wall deliberately excavating to the East (at "Cistern 30") in their newly excavated underground tunnel which runs under the old city. This tunnel extends from the prayer area, Ha Kotel, North towards the Fortress Antonia. Getz hoped to eventually reach the foundation of the Second Temple. During this tunneling, Rabbis Getz and Goren claim to have seen the Ark of the Covenant according to statements they later made to the press. However the Waqf guards on the Temple Mount discovered the underground activity and soon sent down some young men through cistern entrances above to "discourage" the work. A fist fight ensued and the episode concluded with the sealing of the wall with six feet of reinforced cement. The incident was especially tense, as it was not certain at the time whether or not the Jerusalem police had jurisdiction to intervene in the underground excavation since the area was under the jurisdiction of Rabbi Getz. The so-called Rabbinical Tunnel was opened to the public in 1996 as an outstanding new archaeological attraction.

In 1982, after years of disagreement about methods of approach, three groups of devout Jews, The Jerusalem Temple Foundation, To the Mountain of the Lord, and The Faithful of the Temple Mount combined their forces to plan for and build the Third Temple. More recently The Temple Institute has begun to build the sacred vessels to be used in the Third Temple. One yeshiva (Yeshivot Ateret Cohanim) is presently located in the Old City in the historic Torat Haim Yeshiva building. Prior to the Arab riots of 1936, this area of the Old City was a thriving Jewish community. The yeshiva's location places it not far from the spot the Holy of Holies once stood on the Temple Mount.

For a number of years, especially back in the 70's, there were rumors that precut stones have been cut in America and shipped to Israel for the building of the Third Temple. Evangelist John Wesley White wrote:

"Late in 1979 I was riding in Indiana with a local Presbyterian minister. At a certain point along the highway he informed me that we were driving past the gate of a company which purportedly handled a highly classified order of the finest building stones in the world. Sixty thousand tons of pre-cut stones had been shipped on 500 rail cars. They were allegedly bought by the Israeli Government, and had already arrived in Israel."[3]

Such claims are highly unlikely! Anyone who has ever visited Israel will immediately be impressed that stones are everywhere. In fact, Israel actually exports them, and they have the highest quality of pure white limestone in abundance! Whether precut stones have already been made in Israel is another matter. Though rumors abound, no concrete evidence has come forward to support this idea.

During 1982 military action in Lebanon, the Israeli Army discovered and captured huge stores of Russian and Syrian weaponry stored in secret bunkers and tunnels in preparation for a Northern invasion. It was also reported by very reliable sources that a large supply of the famous Lebanese Cedar was also recovered and is safely stored away for use in construction of the Third Temple.

If a new Temple is to be constructed, then there must be a functioning priesthood to perform the proper rites and ceremonies. Such a priesthood is now in the works. In an old stone building in the Old City of Jerusalem, a small group of young scholars is preparing for the building of the Third Temple and the coming of the Messiah.

The founder of one particular yeshiva (school) is Motti Hacohen. Hacohen knew he was a priest, but that never affected his life very much. Until, that is, the day he looked up from his opened Talmud while he was studying at a Yeshiva on the Golan Heights and saw a friend pouring over a tractate dealing with the laws of the temple and the priesthood.

Hacohen asked him why he was studying such obscure laws. His friend responded, "Why aren't you?"

He told Hacohen that he should be more interested in the Temple regulations seeing that he was from the priestly line. Hacohen decided to take up the challenge.

Hacohen then began a search for a yeshiva that could teach him matters concerning the rebuilding of the Temple. Finding none that would satisfy his needs Hacohen founded the Tora Kohanim.

On Good Friday 1990, 150 devout Jews, members of the Yeshivot Ateret Cohanim, moved into four buildings in the Christian quarter of Jerusalem causing a protest from both Muslim and Christian groups. The site of the building, just around the corner from the church of the Holy Sepulcher, was chosen to help create Jewish settlements in the Old City of Jerusalem geographically near the Temple Mount. (The city is presently divided into separate quarters for Christians, Muslims, and Jews and each district's residents are very sensitive to outsiders moving into their territory for any reason).

The problem of restoring the sacrificial system is one that devout Jerusalem Jews have been researching with great zeal and diligence. In an article called, the "Significance of Sacrifice," Jewish writer Pinhas H. Pell writes:

"Ambivalence in regard to the sacrificial cult permeates Jewish thought and literature from the time of the ancient pre-exilic prophets through the Psalms to the rabbis of the Talmud and Midrash and the major medieval philosophers, down to contemporary religious thinkers. It left its imprint on the liturgy and has been (and still is to some extent) the subject of heated debates."

"It is generally thought that sacrifices of life were among the earliest and most profound expressions of the human desire to come as close as possible to God. While in English the verb "to sacrifice" means "to make sacred," the Hebrew word for "sacrifice" (korban, le-hakriv) is from the same root as "to come near, to approach.""

"Sacrifices do indeed present an esthetic, sometimes a moral problem to many modern Jews who are unable to envision being spiritually uplifted at the sight of slaughtered animals, spilled blood and burning incense. Yet, with all the reservations prophets, rabbis and philosophers have expressed about sacrifices, they are indisputably an integral part of Torah legislation, as well as Jewish history in the First and Second Temples and are included in Jewish aspirations concerning the third temple, for whose speedy rebuilding Jews pray daily according to their traditional prayer book."[4]

The Jerusalem Post reports: "The modern Jew found it difficult to face the binding obligation to rebuild the sanctuary, combined with the great dreams linked with it. He has suppressed the demands they make on him.

"He was hesitant to use religious language to describe the historic return to Zion and to national sovereignty. There are indeed a few exceptions to this, as for example, "the Third Temple," once used by Ben-Gurion or the excessive use of prophetic terminology of the "ingathering of the exiles" during the years of mass aliya.

"Far beyond the formal commandment, the yearning to behold an actual concrete expression of a central religious and national focal point permeates all Jewish history.

"Another argument is that the rebuilding as postulated by Maimonides requires a certain order of events: 1) coming to the land; 2) appointment of a king from the house of David; 3) blotting out the descendants of Amalek; and only then 4) the building of the Temple. The counter argument claims that, while this is indeed the ideal order of events, the events themselves are not necessarily mutually interdependent and one must carry out whichever is possible at the time." [5]

Next week Israel's Ministry of Religious Affairs will sponsor a first-ever Conference of Temple Research to discuss whether contemporary Jews are obligated to rebuild the Temple. However, several small organizations in Jerusalem believe the question is settled. They are zealously making preparation for the new Temple in spite of the doctrinal obstacles and the certainty of promoting Muslim fury.

Two Talmudic schools located near the Western

Wall are teaching nearly two hundred students the elaborate details to Temple service. Other groups are researching the family lines of Jewish priests who alone may conduct sacrifices. Former Chief Rabbi Shlomo Goren, who heads another Temple Mount organization, believes his research has fixed the location of the ancient Holy of Holies so that Jews can enter the Mount without sacrilege.

No group is more zealous than the Temple Institute, whose spiritual leader, 50-year-old Rabbi Israel Ariel, was one of the first Israeli paratroopers to reach the Mount in 1967. "Our task," states the institute's American born director, Zev Golan, "is to advance the cause of the Temple and prepare for its establishment, not just talk about it."

One difficulty is the requirement that priest's purify their bodies with the cremated ashes of an unblemished red heifer before they enter the Temple. Following a go-ahead from the Chief Rabbinate, institute operatives spent two weeks in August scouting Europe for heifer embryos that will shortly be implanted into cows at an Israeli cattle ranch.

But historian David Solomon insists that a new Temple is essential: "It was the essence of our Jewish being, the unifying force of our people ... but sooner or later, in a week or a century, it will be done. And we will be ready for it." He adds with quiet urgency, "Every day's delay is a stain on the nation."[6]

According to tradition, no Jew may step foot on the site of the Holy Temple in Jerusalem.

But this week, leading Israeli rabbis, including the former Ashkenazi Chief Rabbi Shlomo Goren ruled that while Jews may not step on holy soil, they are obliged to pray at a sanctuary to be established adjoining the site of the Holy of Holies.

The ruling touched off a storm in Muslim circles. Previously Jews had been forbidden to even enter the Temple Mount. Muslims were allowed total control of the area. The temple Mount includes the Dome of the Rock and the El-Aksa Mosque.

According to Rabbi Goren, a 1967 survey of the Temple Mount shows the exact location of the First and Second Temples as well as the site of the Ark of the Covenant.

By elimination, the rabbi determined the exact areas on the Temple Mount where a Jewish sanctuary could be constructed without violation of the ancient decree not to tread on holy soil.

The synagogue of course would not interfere with Muslim areas of the Mount, Rabbi Goren said.

Earlier efforts by Jews to pray on the Temple Mount touched off clashes with police and Arabs on the Mount. Mayor Teddy Kollek said he feared that Jews praying on the Temple Mount might encounter violence, since Muslims would interpret the Jewish presence as provocation.

But Jews and Muslims conduct prayers side by side at the Cave of Machpeleh in Hebron, site of the tombs of the Patriarchs.

Kollek voiced opposition to the rabbinical action, declaring that "the claim in Jerusalem is a direct result of the 1967 decision not to alter the status of the rights of the various religious groups."

The action by Israel's rabbinate calling for a sanctuary

to be built on the Temple Mount is a religious edict that has the authority of . . . Jewish Law.[7]

The rest of his article and other information can be found at templemount.org.

The Ark of the Covenant

One of the main issues surrounding a Third Temple is the long lost Ark of the Covenant. What will be its place, if any, in the Third Temple? The last mention of the Ark is 2 Chronicles 35:3 where it is placed back into the Temple in the realm of King Josiah. There was no ark in the Second Temple. There is no concrete evidence today that the Ark still exists or that someone has it. Does the Ark exist? If it does will it appear before the Third Temple is consecrated?

Most Orthodox Jewish believers in Jerusalem who are working towards the building of the Third Temple believe that the Ark of the Covenant is safely hidden in a chamber under the Temple Mount. They feel certain God has preserved the Ark for twenty-five centuries and that it will be available when the Temple is restored. The issue of the Ark, its history and present location (if it exists at all) is reserved for a later discussion.

The Ashes of the Red Heifer

Some rabbis claim that one of the things necessary for a Third Temple is the ashes of the Red Heifer. Of all the sacrifices for sin mentioned in the Old Testament, only the slaying of the Red Heifer was "outside the camp," i.e., not in the temple. Numbers chapter 19 describes this offering and gives instructions for preparing water for ritual purification from the ashes of the sacrificed animal after it had been burned.

Red heifers without spot or blemish are today being bred and raised by at least one group in the United States, Rev. Clyde Lott writes in a new 1995 Jewish publication,

The Restoration. [8]

American amateur archaeologist Vendyl Jones of Arlington, Texas, has for many years been searching in caves near Qumran for the ashes of the last red heifer sacrificed before the destruction of the temple in AD 70.

Authorities at The Temple Institute have stated, however, that Third Temple sacrifices and ritual cleansing can be accomplished (restored) without these old ashes if they are not found.

Make sure you check out the website, templeinstitute.org, for current pictures of the ceremonial pieces, priestly garments, harps and other instruments that will be used when the Jews build their temple.

No question about it, we are living in exciting days. We are seeing prophecy come true. We are seeing God's Word fulfilled. Why don't you take a moment to pray this prayer, *Thank You for every prophecy that You have given and how it is coming to pass before my very eyes. Lord, help me to live my life in light of Your soon return.*

CHAPTER 8

The Prosperity

The Upper Room, Jerusalem
Matthew 26

JUDAS SAT AT THE TABLE, EATING UNLEAVENED BREAD AND
DRINKING THE FRUIT OF THE VINE. The lengthening shadows
covered the face that he knew so well but didn't think he
would ever understand. He remembered walking among the
crowds, watching anxious hands pleading for Jesus to stop.
They wanted Him to talk to them, heal them, and comfort
their souls. But his own thought had been of the cool shade
that awaited their band when they stopped for the night. He
planned what he would purchase for their evening meal. He
would take a few extra coins to town; no one would know the
difference. Everyone trusted him.

Why was everyone in the room arguing about which
place they would have in the kingdom? All except Jesus. He
was looking at each face like He would never see it again.
Judas didn't have time for such foolishness, and foolishness
it was. The group was too naïve. He knew that if he had
led the group, he would have done it much differently. He
would have gathered the crowds together in one place and
healed them publicly, asking them to please give an offering
of thanksgiving for the miracle they had just received. It
wouldn't have taken long, and he would have been richer
than his wildest dreams. But now it was time. He was tired
of waiting. *I am a tool*, he thought. *I am ready to be used by
Satan himself.*

He didn't have much time. He hoped the coming

darkness would cover his face. He had carefully masked his expression, but still he knew the miraculous power of their leader. He knew of His power to read their thoughts.

"One of you will betray me," Jesus said.

The words tore at him, flooding his heart with terror. His hands were sweating, and he could hardly keep from clasping them together. He wanted to run away, but he knew that if he did, he would give away his plan. He looked down at his trembling fingers then he looked at Matthew. He was staring at the Lord with a pained expression. His look seemed to reproach the Lord for thinking such a thing of them. He could picture Matthew's feelings for they had to be similar to his own. Didn't Jesus know the sacrifices they had made so far to be with Him? Didn't He know the ridicule they received from their own family members for following a religious fanatic?

Matthew's expression also gave him hope. No one suspected. They all thought they were too good to do anything against the Lord. He picked up a hunk of bread letting his eyes catch the expression on Jesus' face. But then he had to look somewhere else. At even a momentary glance, those eyes bored deeply into him. His hands trembled again. With measured tread, he brought the bread to the oil.

Jesus' hand was already there.

Judas heard Jesus speak then, "The man who dips his bread with me, he is my betrayer."

If he hadn't been sitting on the ground, he would have fallen. The words tore into his innermost being and for a moment he thought, *Why am I going to betray him?* but the idea dissipated almost as soon as it entered his head, for a sudden powerful presence invaded his limbs. His hands which moments before had trembled with fear, now felt strong enough to crush a millstone. His head now felt clear and bright. He wanted the money. Thirty pieces of silver. It wasn't everything he desired, but it was a good start. He stood, looking straight into Jesus' eyes. No longer afraid. It was time. He was a tool, and he was ready.

The command surprised him. "Go quickly. Do the task now."

How did He know so much? Judas faltered for a brief moment as he stood. The other disciples, muttering among themselves about the crowds outside their room, hadn't even noticed the exchange.

He stood now staring. Those eyes. How could He say so much with just His eyes? Again his hesitation vanished. He felt himself once again filled with new strength. He turned and walked toward the door. He opened it purposefully, striding out into the night.

"You are my tool," the voice said, "Obey me."

His master needed him.

* *

WE KNOW FROM SCRIPTURE THAT JUDAS WAS ACTUALLY INDWELT BY SATAN WHEN HE BETRAYED THE LORD. I have often wondered what thoughts passed through Judas' mind as he sat at the Last Supper with Jesus and His disciples. At what point had he made the decision to betray the Lord? We know from earlier Scriptures that when Mary poured her precious ointment on the Lord's feet Judas was angry. He said in John 12:5-6, "Why was not this ointment sold for three hundred pence, and given to the poor? This he said, not that he cared for the poor; but because he was a thief, and had the bag, and bare what was put therein."

So, we know Judas was a thief and probably had been looking for a way to take the money that had been entrusted to him. But there is a far more sinister motivation here than just that Judas was a thief. Satan had been licking his wounds since the Mount of Temptation and the times when Jesus had cast his demons out of people. He was looking for a way to destroy the Son of God, and he saw his opportunity in Judas.

Have you learned in our study so far that Satan is always looking to destroy? Through our study of how he fell from

Heaven, tempted Adam and Eve, hurt Job, tempted David, and tempted Jesus, we see a creature bent on one thing, destruction of all that is good. This was to be Satan's final triumph. Through indwelling Judas, he could bring about the events that would put Christ on the cross. It would be his greatest triumph as the Son of God hung on a criminal cross dying a death that caused every man of that day to shudder.

There is a pattern all through Scripture: every destructive plan of Satan is turned into something God would use for good.

To the world it would look like Christ was finished.
But to us, Christ had to be finished so we could begin anew.
To the world He hung on that cross a defeated King.
But He made it possible for us to enter His Kingdom through the cross.
When He lay in the grave, the world thought He was dead. But in three days, He rose again, proving to that world that He was indeed God.
The world saw defeat. Satan rejoiced but for a moment. In reality, Satan was defeated once and for all.

Yes, Judas was a tool, but he turned out to be simply a part of the greatest defeat of Satan the world has ever known.

Dear friend, as I write these words, I think about how easy it is for us to get discouraged at Satan's tactics. As the Apostle Paul says, oftentimes as believers we are buffeted on every side. Through this study of Satan, I hope you are beginning to understand the true victory that you already possess. I pray that you will look to Jesus and understand that He is greater than any other power in the universe. He will help you no matter what your personal trial.

Perhaps you are feeling discouraged because you are going through a job change or a family adjustment or a financial squeeze. Whatever the case, know this: Satan's greatest triumph turned out to be his greatest defeat. The circumstances you are in may seem bleak, but I beg you to continue to wait on the Lord's provision. He will help you and guide you to victory.

A COMING PROSPERITY

When Satan brings forth his final man, the Antichrist, the world will not at first see his evil side. Just as Judas wasn't suspected of his nefarious scheme, so the Antichrist will at first be accepted as a man whose main desire is to bring peace.

And the place from which he will bring this peace is Babylon.

The Bible talks a lot about Babylon. There are 171 verses that mention this city. It is an important city in God's plan through the ages. There are many differing opinions about the Babylon mentioned in Revelation. Is she a city arising now out of war ravaged Iraq that will become the literal headquarters of the Antichrist? Is there somehow a link that will be formed in the next few years between the United States and Iraq that will bring in a world prosperity thanks to Iraq's oil reserves? Is Babylon the Roman Catholic Church as many scholars including the great Dave Hunt believe? Is Babylon the United States?

While I am not going to take a dogmatic position on this, I believe there is quite a bit of evidence pointing toward the United States being Babylon. The fact that we went to war against Iraq with only strong support from England seems to show that there is going to be a link between our country and Iraq for quite a long time. We could be occupying Iraq for many years though I know this is something that our President doesn't want to do. But with the current anarchy, it seems that only through military occupation can Iraq hope to eventually be ruled by a democracy.

To me it is significant that in the last days, the United States and ancient Babylon are linked. There are many who have said of Iraq that there are vast untouched oil reserves, second only to Saudi Arabia. Imagine how much less we would have to depend on the Saudis if we could count on cheap oil prices from Iraq. This could bring on economic prosperity that would pour money into every sector, changing the current landscape and fulfilling Bible prophecy to the last degree.

ANCIENT BABYLON'S BEGINNING

First, let's look at Babylon's beginning. The Garden of Eden was in the land between the two rivers, the Tigris and Euphrates (Gen. 2:10-11, 13-15). It is amazing that even now, this area of the world is known as the "cradle of civilization" to which scholars throughout the ages have attributed the beginning of the main races of man.

After the worldwide flood, we learn about Nimrod. Nimrod started Babel, the beginning of Babylon. Genesis 10:8-10 states, "And Cush begat Nimrod: he began to be a mighty one in the earth. He was a mighty hunter before the Lord: wherefore it is said, Even as Nimrod the mighty hunter before the Lord. And the beginning of his kingdom was Babel, and Erech, and Accad, and Calneh, in the land of Shinar."

Writer Mark Hitchcock states that "the ancient Hebrew Scriptures also indicate that Nimrod's nature was that of a tyrant, or dictator, you might say that he was the first world dictator, and his capitol city was Babylon."[1]

This implies that even the beginning of Babylon was steeped in arrogance. Of course, we know who the father of pride is, the devil himself.

Remember the famous tower of Babel? This was man's attempt to reach God on his own terms. Once again, the arrogance is astounding, and yet man is sure that he himself holds the answer to his own salvation.

Genesis 11:1-9 tells the story.

And the whole earth was of one language, and of one speech. And it came to pass, as they journeyed from the east, that they found a plain in the land of Shinar; and they dwelt there. And they said one to another,

Go to, let us make brick, and burn them thoroughly. And they had brick for stone, and slime had they for morter. And they said, Go to, let us build us a city and a tower, whose top may reach unto heaven; and let us make us a name, lest we be scattered abroad upon the face of the whole earth. And the Lord came down to see the city and the tower, which the children of men builded. And the Lord said, Behold, the people is one, and they have all one language; and this they begin to do: and now nothing will be restrained from them, which they have imagined to do. Go to, let us go down, and there confound their language, that they may not understand one another's speech. So the Lord scattered them abroad from thence upon the face of all the earth: and they left off to build the city. Therefore is the name of it called Babel; because the Lord did there confound the language of all the earth: and from thence did the Lord scatter them abroad upon the face of all the earth.

From the beginning then we see the religion of Babylon, and we see man's continued attempt to reach God on his own. We see Satan's attempt to make man worship him, and we see that Babylon is far more than just a city in the Bible. It is a philosophy and a religion that has captured the entire world.

Globalism. A new world order. We see both of these things typified at the Tower of Babel. Should we be surprised as it rears its ugly head right in front of us?

THE BABYLONIAN WORLD SYSTEM

One of the main messages of the Bible is regarding the world system that opposes God and His people. This is typified in the Bible by Egypt, Assyria, Medo-Persia, Greece, Rome, and the final system, the revised Roman empire.

Nebuchadnezzar was by far one of the most powerful men the world has ever known. Yet, when we study the

book of Daniel, we see that four young Jewish men who
courageously held true to their upbringing intrigued him.

One night, he had a dream, and it seemed to him that
the dream had some kind of significance beyond his own
understanding. He sent for all of his counselors and advisers
early in the morning and demanded they not only tell him the
meaning of his dream, but also the content of it. Daniel saved
all of the wise men's necks by correctly telling the king his
dream and its meaning. Nebuchadnezzar's dream did have
significance, far greater significance than he could have ever
imagined.

Let's look at that dream in Daniel 2:31-35:

> Thou, O king, sawest, and behold a great image.
> This great image, whose brightness was excellent,
> stood before thee; and the form thereof was terrible.
> This image's head was of fine gold, his breast and
> his arms of silver, his belly and his thighs of brass,
> His legs of iron, his feet part of iron and part of clay.
> Thou sawest till that a stone was cut out without
> hands, which smote the image upon his feet that were
> of iron and clay, and brake them to pieces. Then was
> the iron, the clay, the brass, the silver, and the gold,
> broken to pieces together, and became like the chaff
> of the summer threshingfloors; and the wind carried
> them away, that no place was found for them: and the
> stone that smote the image became a great mountain,
> and filled the whole earth.

What did this dream mean? The four metals in the
great statue represented four empires that would appear
successively on the world scene to rule over the civilized
world of that day. We now know from looking back at history
that these four empires were Babylon, Medo-Persia, Greece,
and Rome. The feet and ten toes of iron and clay point
forward to a final, ten-king form of the Roman Empire.

The great stone cut without hands represents the Lord
Jesus Christ. He will destroy the Antichrist and his kingdom

at His Second Coming, and then He will set up His own kingdom that will fill the whole earth.

Historically, it is easy to see why God characterized Nebuchadnezzar's kingdom as that of gold. Prophecy researcher, Charles H. Dyer wrote this, "The historian Herodotus visited Babylon about one hundred years after Nebuchadnezzar and reported that he had never in his life seen such a proliferation and abundance of gold. One statue of the god Marduk alone weighed twenty-two tons [that's 44,000 pounds!] of solid gold."[2]

As each subsequent kingdom came into power, they were less powerful than the gold kingdom. But historians agree that these have been the kingdoms that have ruled the earth. These are the kingdoms who can say they were a "world power."

There is no real world power today except the United States.

I don't say this because I am a citizen of this country. I say this because it is true. While other countries have power, the United States has led the world in almost every area. If you read even recent books about prophecy (I read over 100 in preparation for this book), most of them characterize the United States as going down in power, as slowly losing her resources. Many prophecy scholars see the European nations as the coming power that would rule the world. And while in many ways, I see that coming, I also see that the United States isn't going down in power at all, at least for the present. We didn't get humiliated in Iraq as the media predicted. While our economy has been down, there are signs that it is recovering. The European nations now want to get a slice of the pie in Iraq, wanting building contracts and cheap oil.

Worldwatch Institute states this, "Although Iraq's immense oil fields survived the recent war with relatively minor damage, the process of reintegrating Iraq into the world oil market will likely prove more problematic. Iraq's oil can provide the financial resources to rebuild the nation's economy," says Christopher Flavin, the Institute's president. "But an internal or external struggle to control that oil could derail efforts to revitalize Iraq. It is a sad geopolitical fact that of the dozen major exporters of oil, only Norway has a stable and representative political system. Everywhere else, the concentrated, easily extracted wealth that oil provides has led to dictatorships, corruption, and continued poverty for most citizens."

Iraq has produced roughly 2.5 million barrels of oil per day in recent years, making it the world's twelfth largest producer. But Iraq has the second largest proven reserves, 112.5 billion barrels, second only to Saudi Arabia, and more than three times that of the United States.

I don't see the United States becoming insignificant at all. In fact, if anything I see the United States growing in its importance to the world.

BETTER BEFORE IT GETS WORSE

Revelation states that the economic situation of the world will get better before it gets worse. Understand that by better I don't mean by God's standards. Rather I mean the world that has swallowed Satan's lie of materialism. I believe there is evidence in Revelation and Daniel that there will be a general peace and prosperity as the Antichrist begins his rule. Remember, the Antichrist takes the kingdoms of the world with peace, not with force (Daniel 11:21) and later the nations will weep when a prosperous Superpower is destroyed (Rev. 14:7-8). There is nothing to weep for if there was no peace and prosperity to begin with. This peace lulls the world to sleep and keeps her from understanding what is happening. A peace that dulls the conscience and causes people to say, "Where is the sign of the Lord's coming? When is He going to come back anyway?" Dear friend, when you hear people saying these things, know this, the Lord's return is closer at hand than ever before. Their disbelieving words prove that God has been right all along.

WILL BABYLON BE REBUILT IN IRAQ?

Will Babylon, the actual city in Iraq, be rebuilt? We know that while Saddam Hussein was in power, he made a token attempt to rebuild the ancient city that King Nebuchadnezzar once ruled. Yet, Saddam's Babylon is far from becoming a functioning city. His version of the famous city is just a few buildings, which might make a nice tourist stop even today. I certainly would love to see it. Charles Dyer's book about Babylon contains pictures of Saddam's rebuilt city, and it is exciting to note that there are still bricks in the city that have Nebuchadnezzar's name on them. I thought about that as thousands of our troops flooded Iraq. Would their curiosity get a hold of them as they trekked through cities with biblical names? Would they begin studying the Bible because of it? I believe in the last days that God is supplying more and more evidence of His power and might, showing again and again that the world is without excuse.

Many Christian leaders believe that a new, rebuilt Babylon will become the Antichrist's center of political power. The *Left Behind* series indicates this in the fictional account of what will happen to the world after the Rapture.

Babylon could be rebuilt and it might become a major political power, but I seriously doubt that will happen without a lot of help from the United States. So who would be the real Babylon then?

Take a moment to read through the three main verses that people believe say Babylon, the actual city in Iraq, must be rebuilt.

Jeremiah 50:1-3 states, "The word that the Lord spake against Babylon and against the land of the Chaldeans by Jeremiah the prophet. Declare ye among the nations, and publish, and set up a standard; publish, and conceal not: say, Babylon is taken, Bel is confounded, Merodach is broken in pieces; her idols are confounded, her images are broken in pieces. For out of the north there cometh up a nation against her, which shall make her land desolate, and none shall dwell therein: they shall remove, they shall depart, both man and beast."

Jeremiah 51:47-48 says, "Therefore, behold, the days come, that I will do judgment upon the graven images of Babylon: and her whole land shall be confounded, and all her slain shall fall in the midst of her. Then the heaven and the earth, and all that is therein, shall sing for Babylon: for the spoilers shall come unto her from the north, saith the Lord."

Revelation 18:2-12 tells us more about the wealth of this country,

> And he cried mightily with a strong voice, saying, Babylon the great is fallen, is fallen, and is become the habitation of devils, and the hold of every foul spirit, and a cage of every unclean and hateful bird. For all nations have drunk of the wine of the wrath of her fornication, and the kings of the earth have committed fornication with her, and the merchants of the earth are waxed rich through the abundance of her delicacies. And I heard another voice from heaven, saying, Come out of her, my people, that ye be not partakers of her sins, and that ye receive not of her plagues. For her sins have reached unto heaven, and God hath remembered her iniquities. Reward her even as she rewarded you, and double unto her double according to her works: in the cup which she hath filled fill to her double. How much she hath glorified herself, and lived deliciously, so much torment and sorrow give her: for she saith in her heart, I sit a queen, and am no widow, and shall see no sorrow. Therefore shall her plagues come in one day, death, and mourning, and famine; and she shall be utterly burned with fire: for strong is the Lord God who judgeth her. And the kings of the earth, who have committed fornication and lived deliciously with her, shall bewail her, and lament for her, when they shall see the smoke of her burning, Standing afar off for

the fear of her torment, saying, Alas, alas, that great city Babylon, that mighty city! for in one hour is thy judgment come. And the merchants of the earth shall weep and mourn over her; for no man buyeth their merchandise any more: The merchandise of gold, and silver, and precious stones, and of pearls, and fine linen, and purple, and silk, and scarlet, and all thine wood, and all manner vessels of ivory, and all manner vessels of most precious wood, and of brass, and iron, and marble.

We are told in Scripture that the Antichrist will sign a peace treaty with Israel, and he will declare himself to be God in the temple in Jerusalem. The Beast will try to defeat Christ as He returns to the Holy City. The only commentary we read about Babylon describes its destruction.

Terry James, owner of the Raptureready website says this, "One of the strongest arguments against the possibility that the city of Babylon will be rebuilt is based on Revelation 18 that we just read. This passage says that when the city is destroyed, the merchants of the world will mourn its destruction as a great financial loss. We could very easily apply this prophecy to a city like New York, but for now, there is no way we could honestly say this about any city in Iraq."

I tend to agree. In my mind, it is easy to apply this idea of merchants mourning because America has fallen during the Tribulation period. Who has made the nations of the world rich? Who has ruined the nations of the world because of her dirty movies? Who has enjoyed some of the highest living standards in the history of the world?

Of course, America has. It is difficult at this time to see Iraq making the nations of the world rich. If anything, Iraq has hurt the nations of the world financially.

For the last ten years, many people have looked to the United Nations or the European Common Market as the coming world power, and while I believe both of these entities will play a role in the end times, I don't think we can look at the current world situation and see the United States fading from the world scene.

I find it interesting that America and Britain ended up going into Iraq by themselves during our last war. We didn't wait for a second resolution from the United Nations. Our enemies say we acted impetuously and arrogantly and yet, we went in and won the war in just three weeks. What kind of effect will this victory have on the world in the coming years? As I mentioned before, this could be a fulfillment of Bible prophecy in the sense that Iraq is now "joined" with the United States.

WAS BABYLON DESTROYED?

The reason scholars say that the ancient city of Babylon must be rebuilt is because they feel it wasn't actually destroyed in the past. Here is a passage they use for that scenario.

Isaiah 13:19-22 says,

> And Babylon, the glory of kingdoms, the beauty of the Chaldees' excellency, shall be as when God overthrew Sodom and Gomorrah. It shall never be inhabited, neither shall it be dwelt in from generation to generation: neither shall the Arabian pitch tent there; neither shall the shepherds make their fold there. But wild beasts of the desert shall lie there; and their houses shall be full of doleful creatures; and owls shall dwell there, and satyrs shall dance there. And the wild beasts of the islands shall cry in their desolate houses, and dragons in their pleasant palaces: and her time is near to come, and her days shall not be prolonged.

The contention is that Babylon still hasn't been totally destroyed, although many times it has been conquered. They say this in spite of the fact that many Arabs today won't pitch their tents in the ancient ruins of the city and in spite of the fact that although Saddam Hussein built his own interpretation of Babylon over the ruins of the city itself, his own palace isn't on the ancient ruins at all, rather it is to the side of the city, overlooking it.

Even Saddam Hussein, when he was in his greatest glory, didn't want to dwell in Babylon.

Prophecy scholars also use a verse from Jeremiah concerning Babylon's bricks.

Jeremiah 51:24-26 says, "And I will render unto Babylon and to all the inhabitants of Chaldea all their evil that they have done in Zion in your sight, saith the Lord. Behold, I am against thee, O destroying mountain, saith the Lord, which destroyest all the earth: and I will stretch out mine hand upon thee, and roll thee down from the rocks, and will make thee a burnt mountain. And they shall not take of thee a stone for a corner, nor a stone for foundations; but thou shalt be desolate for ever, saith the Lord."

Is this prophecy speaking of ancient Babylon or is it speaking of the Babylon mentioned in Revelation? I believe that Babylon was destroyed. Remember Jesus prophesied this of the temple, "And Jesus said unto them, See ye not all these things? verily I say unto you, There shall not be left here one stone upon another, that shall not be thrown down" (Mat. 24:2).

Yet, according to the *Encyclopedia Britannica*, there were stones enough to build a temple to Jupiter on the temple mount.[3]

We know this: Ancient Babylon was destroyed. We know that even the Arabs don't like to spend the night there now. It is easy to see that Babylon in Revelation boasts of the satanic philosophies of the ancient one, but it also clearly has worldwide influence. That is why I believe Babylon could be the United States.

Note I said "could." As I mentioned before, this isn't a doctrine I am willing to die for. Yet, I believe that in looking at our current world situation, it is a reasonable assumption, especially in light of our recent war with Iraq.

Jews Living in Babylon

Allow me to ask you a question, how many Jews are living in
Iraq today? Not many. Since Muslim thought for many years
has dominated Iraq, Jewish people aren't exactly welcome
there. There are many verses in Scripture that say that many
Jews will come out of "Babylon" before it is destroyed. Let's
look at a few of them.

Jeremiah 50:8 states, "Remove out of the midst of
Babylon, and go forth out of the land of the Chaldeans, and
be as the he goats before the flocks."

Jeremiah 51:6 explains, "Flee out of the midst of
Babylon, and deliver every man his soul: be not cut off in
her iniquity; for this is the time of the Lord's vengeance; he
will render unto her a recompence."

Revelation 18:4 says, "And I heard another voice from
heaven, saying, Come out of her, my people, that ye be
not partakers of her sins, and that ye receive not of her
plagues."

The Jews are encouraged to come out of Babylon, but if
there are no Jews in Babylon, then how can they flee?

The Hebrew University in Jerusalem states on its website,
"Geographical mobility and the increased fragmentation
of the global system of nations notwithstanding, over 80
percent of world Jewry live in two countries, the United
States and Israel, and 95 percent are concentrated in ten
countries." The National Jewish Population Survey found
in September 2003 that Jewish population has dropped 5
percent down to 5.2 million living in the United States.
4,847,000 is the number of Jews living in Israel according to
the Jewish Virtual Library with the next comparable country
being France with 600,000 then Russia with 550,000. Italy
has 35,000 and Iran is listed as having 25,000. Iraq ties Tahiti
with the smallest number of Jews at less than 120 in each.

The Deep Water Ports Issue

Revelation 18:17-19 tells of merchant ships standing off the shoreline of Babylon. The ships have either just unloaded or are waiting to dock when the terrible judgment comes. The ships, the captains, crew, and passengers witness the destruction.

Take a moment to read this description now.

"For in one hour so great riches is come to nought. And every shipmaster, and all the company in ships, and sailors, and as many as trade by sea, stood afar off, And cried when they saw the smoke of her burning, saying, What city is like unto this great city! And they cast dust on their heads, and cried, weeping and wailing, saying, Alas, alas, that great city, wherein were made rich all that had ships in the sea by reason of her costliness! for in one hour is she made desolate."

How could this occur in Babylon today? The Euphrates River is their main waterway, but the one small gulf isn't exactly a deep water port. How did the United States and Britain take over Iraq? Air power. Iraq is also not a merchandising capital of the world as this passage indicates. And of course, we know this isn't true of Rome either. While I believe Rome is part of the spiritual Babylon, I believe only the United States fits when it comes to commerce.

A Rich Nation Who Makes Others Rich

Revelation 18:3 says, "For all nations have drunk of the wine of the wrath of her fornication, and the kings of the earth have committed fornication with her, and the merchants of the earth are waxed rich through the abundance of her delicacies." What other rich nation has brought prosperity to other nations like the United States? Why is the US considered the melting pot? Because people from all over the world have come here with dreams of a better life. Through our commerce and trade, we have made other nations rich.

I have traveled the world extensively and held crusades in India that number in the thousands and have seen the power of the American dollar. It is generally preferred above any other currency. The English language is also considered the universal language. For the most part, if you speak English, you can go anywhere and do anything. Hollywood and our rock music have also corrupted the world far beyond anything we can imagine. Even in the poorest street of India, I've heard people listening to our rock music.

Muslim countries hate our western culture. They have strict laws prohibiting their women from wearing our clothing, and they condemn our movies and television. We don't see the Muslim countries invading the world's culture. Rather we see them withdrawing into themselves and supporting only each other.

THE POLICEMAN OF THE WORLD

Babylon is referred to as the hammer of the whole earth in Jeremiah 50:23: "How is the hammer of the whole earth cut asunder and broken! how is Babylon become a desolation among the nations!"

The words "hammer of the whole earth" imply that Babylon is considered the world's policeman. Now, is Iraq considered the world's policeman? Since even before the break up of the Soviet Union, America was known as the world force politically willing to help other nations keep peace. Even the United Nations, a collection of nations formed to keep peace in the world, is based in New York. The United States plays a huge role in the United Nations.

Our recent war with Iraq is a classic example of this. While we called this a "war against terrorism," George Bush mentioned that the people of Iraq were now free of a terrible dictator who had only desired to hurt them.

While in a taxicab in Switzerland, the cabdriver told me that he didn't like George Bush because he was from Texas, a state known for its executions of criminals. George Bush has been called the Cowboy Policeman by the media for years, and while I do not agree with this perception of our President, it shows what the world thinks of us as a country.

While I would never wish the destruction foretold in Revelation 17 and 18 on the United States, I believe there is evidence that indeed we could be the last Superpower, that we can look toward a period of extreme prosperity before the Rapture. This doesn't mean I rejoice in a coming prosperity—the true church has always done better through times of persecution. When people have material riches heaped upon them, they are less likely to consider their need for the Lord.

Will ancient Babylon be rebuilt or will the United States and Babylon grow side by side creating economic wealth before their eventual fall? I know one thing for sure, Babylon is a tool in the hand of God to bring judgment. It is a nation that has corrupted the nations of the world with material wealth and wickedness. When she is destroyed, the world will weep.

There is a reason Babylon is called a mystery. But it is a mystery that will soon be revealed.

CHAPTER 9

The Seal

Jerusalem
Acts 4:36-5:16

SATAN STRUCK HIS HANDS TOGETHER. This new church was different than anything God had done so far. The people were united in common goals.

The new seal was a constant reminder of their standing before God. Sensing the Spirit's presence more than he ever had before, he watched as the people kneeled asking the Creator for His blessing on their witnessing endeavors.

This group didn't need any more help, especially when Barnabas just sold some of his land.

Satan hated this disregard for their own possessions or even their lives. Greed had always been an easy tool for him to use.

He had watched this growing assembly for several days. Singing, caring, giving to each other, bestowing the surplus to the street people, loving each other, talking in glowing tones about their Savior, Jesus.

Jesus. The name continued to haunt him in the night. He had lost the battle just when he thought he had won.

He couldn't believe it. Judas had done such a superb job of bringing Jesus to justice. At the last minute Satan had sensed a slight ambivalence and so had felt it was necessary to indwell Judas, but otherwise his man had performed well.

Satan had delighted in the trial and the people's apparent

eagerness to torment Jesus. But it had also seemed too easy. Jesus hadn't resisted. He didn't defend himself at the trial either. He had simply answered their questions.

Satan didn't think he expected Jesus to slay them all or bring down legions of angels or masses of fire from Heaven, but he was surprised that God the Father let His Son go . . . so willingly.

When the nails went into His hands and feet, all of the demon underlings clapped and cheered, but Satan had begun to think something was amiss. Why was this so easy? You would have thought Jesus needed to die and was using Satan's orchestration to accomplish His Father's will.

The idea was absurd, but it stuck with him for three days.

Today he understood more than he had ever wanted to know. When Jesus burst from the tomb, he felt a deep dread.

Jesus was alive. But He was supposed to be finished.

Now it seemed like Jesus wasn't finished at all. His trembling, stupid followers had taken on new life, shouting from the rooftops that Jesus was the Son of God.

The cross hadn't banished Jesus at all.

Satan knew he would continue looking for his man, the one who would fool the earth forever.

But until then, the man in row three was a good pick. Satan had seen his look when Barnabas came forward with a pile of money.

He knew Ananias was greedy.

As simple as picking a ripe pomegranate from a tree. If only Jesus had been so easy.

* *

SATAN INDEED FOUND WILLING ACCOMPLICES IN ANANIAS AND HIS WIFE SAPPHRIA. Ananias did a worthy thing in selling his property, but then did a vile thing in saying he had brought all the money as a gift to the church when in fact he had kept back part of it. Ananias was killed as an example to all. A few hours later, his wife Sapphria lied, and she was killed.

Instead of Ananias and Sapphria's deed being a tool of Satan, their deed became a warning. Fear fell on that congregation as they realized again that they served the true and the living God.

In this study of Satan and his coming man, I'm sure you have noticed one ruling characteristic. Just when Satan thinks he's won, he finds himself thwarted again. It must be disconcerting to find that every plan you have is part of a bigger, master plan enacted by the Creator Himself.

Not one plan of Satan has succeeded or ever will succeed.

In the end, only God's plan works.

Which brings us to another phase of the Tribulation, in which we see God's mercy meted out in a powerful way.

One preacher said, "We see multitudes that can't be numbered come to God during the very worst period of human history, saved while in the jaws of death and tottering on the very brink of Hell. That is the love of God."

God's compassion in the midst of God's judgment. Why aren't we surprised? We have a God who delights in giving us second, third, and more chances.

He seals 144,000 Jewish men to prove it.

Imagine for a moment with me the following: Dark days. Plagues. Earthquakes. Torment. Mothers, fathers, sisters, brothers, the elderly, all running from their ruined homes searching for haven and not finding it. This world which had seemed on the brink of new prosperity and peace is crumbling all around them. There seems nowhere to go, nowhere to turn.

They hide. They tremble. They wonder if the world is coming to an end. In the midst of all this confusion, God shows His unfailing mercy. Thousands of perfectly trained evangelists, who possess a strong desire to share the gospel, who love the lost, and who are commissioned by God Himself to go all over the world to evangelize. They have God's name on their foreheads. This is in stark contrast to those who have 666 on their foreheads or on their hand.

This is their seal, their mark of identification. The world has its seal too in Satan's counterfeit number 666. Never have the two sides been drawn more starkly.

As these men evangelize, events are unfolding around them that are the exact fulfillment of events predicted in Daniel and Revelation. When one of the evangelists talks, he simply reads portions of Revelation, and people will think he is reading a current newspaper. There will be much less need for faith as we know it today. The events unfolding will be so obvious and clear that people will either believe God or believe Satan's lie. This is one of the reasons taking the mark of the beast is such a sign of choosing to believe Satan's lie. Everything will be so obvious that people won't be able to waffle about their decision anymore.

That's why when people take the mark of the beast there is no second chance. They are declaring their choice to the world. But many people will trust Christ. Many thousands will die for that decision.

FAITHFUL'S REWARD

My daughter, Julie, has been reading *Little Pilgrim's Progress*, to her two children, James (8) and Amanda (6). This book is a child's version of the John Bunyan classic, *Pilgrim's Progress*. In the course of the story, the main character, Christian, goes through many difficulties on his journey to the Celestial City. Along the way he meets a friend named Faithful. Just as his name implies, Faithful is not only a faithful friend to Christian, but also a steadfast believer. When they reach a riotous city named Vanity Fair, Faithful and Christian are taken captive and ridiculed for their faith. James and Amanda were glued to Julie's reading at this point, wondering what was going to happen to the boys. Christian and Faithful are both beaten but Faithful is burned at the stake. Just at the end, when Christian is crying uncontrollably for his friend, the Lord lets Christian see a beautiful chariot and angels who gather up his friend and take him on to the Celestial City. This vision comforts Christian as he continues on his journey.

Amanda said later, "Mom, I'd like to be like Faithful in the story."

Julie didn't quite know what to say to this. She understandably doesn't want to see her precious daughter martyred for Christ.

"Why is that, Amanda?" she asked.

"Because Faithful got to go ahead of Christian to the Celestial City. He had a lot of fun when he got there, I'm sure."

Aren't children precious in how they view life? They see life like we should see it. Amanda's view of Faithful is that while he had some hard times, in the end, he got to Heaven ahead of Christian. This is what will happen during the Tribulation. There will be many people who listen to the 144,000 and trust Christ. Most of those will be rewarded for their faith with martyrdom. But they will be in Heaven praising God for those wonderful evangelists who led them to Christ.

TIME OUT FOR MERCY

Take a few minutes to read Revelation 7,

> And after these things I saw four angels standing on the four corners of the earth, holding the four winds of the earth, that the wind should not blow on the earth, nor on the sea, nor on any tree. And I saw another angel ascending from the east, having the seal of the living God: and he cried with a loud voice to the four angels, to whom it was given to hurt the earth and the sea, Saying, Hurt not the earth, neither the sea, nor the trees, till we have sealed the servants of our God in their foreheads. And I heard the number of them which were sealed: and there were sealed an hundred and forty and four thousand of all the tribes of the children of Israel. Of the tribe

of Juda were sealed twelve thousand. Of the tribe of
Reuben were sealed twelve thousand. Of the tribe
of Gad were sealed twelve thousand. Of the tribe
of Aser were sealed twelve thousand. Of the tribe
of Nepthalim were sealed twelve thousand. Of the
tribe of Manasses were sealed twelve thousand. Of
the tribe of Simeon were sealed twelve thousand. Of
the tribe of Levi were sealed twelve thousand. Of the
tribe of Issachar were sealed twelve thousand. Of the
tribe of Zabulon were sealed twelve thousand. Of
the tribe of Joseph were sealed twelve thousand. Of
the tribe of Benjamin were sealed twelve thousand.
After this I beheld, and, lo, a great multitude, which
no man could number, of all nations, and kindreds,
and people, and tongues, stood before the throne,
and before the Lamb, clothed with white robes, and
palms in their hands; And cried with a loud voice,
saying, Salvation to our God which sitteth upon the
throne, and unto the Lamb. And all the angels stood
round about the throne, and about the elders and the
four beasts, and fell before the throne on their faces,
and worshipped God, Saying, Amen: Blessing, and
glory, and wisdom, and thanksgiving, and honour,
and power, and might, be unto our God for ever and
ever. Amen. And one of the elders answered, saying
unto me, What are these which are arrayed in white
robes? and whence came they? And I said unto him,
Sir, thou knowest. And he said to me, These are they
which came out of great tribulation, and have washed
their robes, and made them white in the blood of the
Lamb. Therefore are they before the throne of God,
and serve him day and night in his temple: and he
that sitteth on the throne shall dwell among them.
They shall hunger no more, neither thirst any more;
neither shall the sun light on them, nor any heat. For
the Lamb which is in the midst of the throne shall
feed them, and shall lead them unto living fountains

of waters: and God shall wipe away all tears from their eyes.

These verses are powerful. Every time I read them, I have to wipe tears from my own eyes. Several years ago when I preached through Revelation, I memorized several chapters, and this was a chapter I learned by heart. To think of this huge group of people who were slain for His name awes my soul.

Why don't you take a moment and thank God for including this group of special people in the Tribulation period? Thank Him for a continuing picture of His grace and mercy in the midst of well-deserved judgment. Then think back on your own life. Are there instances where you saw the grace of the Lord? Perhaps you came close to having a traffic accident, or you were involved in an accident but you survived. It could be that God delivered you from an addiction to drugs or alcohol. Maybe you have seen a parent or loved one soften toward the Lord when once they refused to hear anything about Him. Whatever your particular situation, I encourage you to thank Him for His grace right now. Because even in the midst of the worst judgment, the 144,000 are a sign of mercy.

NO PLACE TO HIDE

Can you imagine having a seal on your forehead that proclaims to all that you are a Christian? Would that change how you act in certain situations? The 144,000 will have a seal that unequivocally states that they are Christians. Everyone will know. There will be no closet Christians during the Tribulation.

Meet Andrew. His home was recently demolished in an earthquake leaving him with little but the clothes on his back. But he doesn't care. In fact, he hasn't thought about the loss of his earthly possessions for several months now.

That's because Andrew now has a new purpose. He is one of the 144,000. When he passes a shop window and sees his reflection, he also notices a mark on his forehead. Thankfully, it doesn't say 666. Rather it is the seal, his own special seal that he has a purpose on this earth.

Everyone who knows Andrew can't help but listen to him. Part of it is because of Andrew's contagious enthusiasm and fervor, but part of it also is because of his seal.

Now picture what would happen if during a moment of weakness, Andrew walked into a movie theater. The people around him would immediately become uncomfortable with him. I have to admit that my imagination goes a little wild when I think of this. What if Andrew's seal started shining brighter and brighter until the people sitting around him couldn't see their movie?

Can you envision how embarrassed Andrew would feel? When he walked out of the theater, there might be people who would never trust what Andrew had to say because of his poor testimony that day. Understand that Andrew is fictitious. I don't know the names of any of these future evangelists. But I do know this. Their seals will mark them as different. Their seals will keep them separated from the world. Their seals will authenticate their words and cause them to be listened to.

Dear friend, do you realize that you and I have a seal as well? The Bible says that we are sealed with the Holy Spirit as believers. We have Almighty God dwelling within us, the Creator of the Heavens and Earth. And yet, many times we don't understand just how precious and wonderful this is. It is just as breathtaking as having a visible seal on our foreheads, even more spectacular because the Bible promises that the Holy Spirit is there to guide us and lead us into all truth.

Do we really understand what a privilege it is to have the seal? Do we take this seriously enough? Do you realize how much we undermine the message of the gospel when we do things that dishonor the Lord?

All of us can determine to take our seal more seriously. All of us can ask the Holy Spirit to lead and guide us. We should thank God for giving us this precious gift.

All of us need to understand the importance of our seal. The 144,000 will.

WHO ARE THE 144K?

There are many theories as to who the 144K are. The Seventh-Day Adventists apply it to the faithful who will be found observing the Jewish Sabbath at the Lord's return. The Jehovah Witnesses believe that "the wise servant" which Jesus speaks in Matthew 24:45 refers to a servant class of people, the "144,000 elect" particularly the ones living at Watchtower headquarters in Bethel, who dispense what they call the "true food of God" (by which they mean their "proper interpretation" of the Word and will of God) to over 10 million Jehovah's Witnesses.[1] According to this teaching, all humankind both male, and female will make up this body. Of course, the problem is that the Bible is clear that the 144K are all male.

Many religious groups throughout the years have taken this number and applied it to themselves. The main problem with this teaching is that the Bible is also clear that the 144K were from the twelve tribes of Israel (12,000 from each tribe). The 144K are also given a specific time in which they are to minister, which is in the Tribulation period. Any group ascribing this number to themselves is definitely missing the meaning of Scripture.

The late preacher Ray Stedman said this in a sermon about the 144K,

> I have deliberately read the names of each of the tribes because I want to emphasize what the text emphasizes: It is Israel and only Israel that is in view! I recently listened to a commentator on Revelation, teaching on the radio here in the Bay Area, who labored with diligent effort to prove that these people were the church, but when God says Israel He means Israel; He does not mean the church. He is talking about Jews. Teachers who twist Scripture like that

man did can convince others that black is white, sugar is sour, and Adolph Hitler was one of the great saints of all time! There is much such twisting of Scripture going on, but if one stays with the simplicity of the Scripture itself, all is clear. These are, then, the well-known 144,000 Jews of the last days.

This passage reinforces the fact that God is not done with the nation of Israel and that He always has a remnant.

WORLDWIDE REVIVAL

The response to the 144K's evangelistic efforts is overwhelming. We see that they are able to bring forth the greatest revival in history. This revival will exceed the Day of Pentecost, the Reformation in Europe, and the Great Awakening in America in numbers of souls coming to know the Lord. I heard a staff member with Friends of Israel, Andrew Ferrier, mention that he believes that the number of souls saved during this time will be greater than the number of souls that have been saved since the day of Pentecost.

How do we know this? Look back at verse nine. Revelation 7:9 states, "After this I beheld, and, lo, a great multitude, which no man could number, of all nations, and kindreds, and people, and tongues, stood before the throne, and before the Lamb, clothed with white robes, and palms in their hands."

This group is distinct from the 144K. This is the evangelized group. Notice that it says a multitude that no man could number of all nations, all people, and all races. The 144K could obviously be numbered. This group cannot be. Many scholars suggest that this is the same group John saw under the altar later in Revelation. This is the group that is then martyred, entering into their rest as mentioned in the fifth seal.

I know one thing for sure, this will be the revival to end all revivals. Remember when Jesus said that all the angels in Heaven rejoice when one sinner repents? Imagine the excitement and joy in Heaven as all these souls come to Christ. Tears come to my eyes just thinking about it, for there is nothing in this world I delight in more than for people to trust Christ.

We will meet them again when we come to Chapter 20. There we are told, "And I saw thrones, and they sat upon them, and judgment was given unto them: and I saw the souls of them that were beheaded for the witness of Jesus, and for the word of God, and which had not worshipped the beast, neither his image, neither had received his mark upon their foreheads, or in their hands; and they lived and reigned with Christ a thousand years" (Rev. 20:4). John sees them in heaven at this point, but they are given a spiritual ministry on earth during the thousand-year reign of Christ. That is suggested in the closing description of their ministry, beginning with Revelation 7:15.

As I studied this passage I thought about the reaction of these people to being in front of the throne of God. Their lips sing only praise. They are thrilled to be a part of this great assembly. Their troubles on earth are forgotten, and the Lamb gives wonderful promises to them about their future in Heaven. You don't see this group lamenting their martyrdom saying, "Oh Lord, we regret what we did for you!" Instead we see them blessing and praising the Lord, thanking Him for His eternal salvation.

PROMISES FOR YOU

Consider these promises for a moment:
1. They are before the throne of God
2. They serve Him day and night in His Temple
3. God will spread His tent over them
4. Never again will they hunger
5. Never again will they thirst
6. The sun will not beat upon them
7. Nor will any scorching heat
8. The Lamb will be their Shepherd

9. He will lead them to springs of living water
10. God will wipe away every tear from their eyes

What joy these words must have brought to this vast multitude that had known such hardship on earth. Even one or two of these promises would be wonderful, but they could count on all ten and more.

Sometimes as we face trials and problems here on this earth, we are tempted to think, "I am doing so much for the Lord. I hope He appreciates it." Of course, we would never speak these words out loud, but sometimes we think them. Yet, when I consider the response of the vast multitude evangelized by the 144K praising and blessing God in spite of the fact that they were just martyred for their faith, it gives me a new perspective. It helps me see life right now with my eternal glasses instead of my temporary ones. No matter what hardship we face on this earth, it will be nothing compared to the glory that awaits us in Heaven.

You see, dear friend, all the promises given to the multitude in this passage will also be given to you. When you get to Heaven you will never again cry because you will have nothing to cry about, everything will be perfect. You will enjoy the presence of the Lord to an extent you can only dream of now. You will never have any more pain or sickness or contacts or diabetes or heart diseases or cancer or arthritis. Don't these thoughts make you excited about Heaven? Don't these thoughts bring you to a new understanding of what the Christian life is like?

Paul wrote this, "For our light affliction, which is but for a moment, worketh for us a far more exceeding and eternal weight of glory; While we look not at the things which are seen, but at the things which are not seen: for the things which are seen are temporal; but the things which are not seen are eternal" (2 Cor. 4:17-18).

Are you looking at the eternal or are you looking at right now? Are you tempted to gripe about your problems? None of us enjoys problems and trials, but if we look at them from an eternal perspective, when we get to Heaven, all our problems are going to turn into praise. All our trials will fade away and will be no more.

So, why don't we turn our problems into praise right now? Is there a difficulty in your life such as an unsaved spouse, a cranky boss, or a controlling mother-in-law? Perhaps you face daily difficulties from diabetes or another illness, as I do. Whatever the situation, take this opportunity to look to Heaven. Picture yourself around the throne praising the Lord. You'll find your problems will look a lot different when you are finished.

Chapter 10

The Witnesses

Jerusalem
Revelation 11

THE TEMPLE WAS FINALLY FINISHED. The jubilation celebration was about to begin and his man was going to appear and cut the ribbon. He watched the camera crews jockey each other for the best position at the court of the Gentiles. Armed guards kept back the Jewish masses wanting to worship and sacrifice. It was a strange sight in the 21st century to see sheep jostling about with the people. Someone had dressed up one lamb in a white satin outfit, complete with leather boots. At first no one had believed that the world would accept animal sacrifices, but when the Arab countries agreed to tolerate the temple in exchange for the rest of the city, public opinion had decided that sacrificing sheep was better than sacrificing men, women, and children to the terrors of a seemingly endless supply of suicide bombers.

It was all part of the plan. Destroy the Jews and drive them into the sea. The mantra had become a secret war cry for the false Jewish peace. From every part of the world the Jews would come, to see their temple and to rejoice on its opening day. Now, they could all be destroyed at once.

He looked over the crowd from his perch on a wall noticing two men wearing what looked like coarse rags sewn together. Their long white beards blended in with the many Hassidic Jews gathered around but it was their eyes that caught his attention. The one man's were deep aquamarine, the other's a vivid emerald. They assessed the crowd and while he knew they couldn't see him, for a moment, he felt as though they could. They stood by a decorative fountain that was shooting streams of water into the air to the pulsating music.

Who were these men? What were they doing here?

Suddenly he heard a collective gasp and a woman's scream. Streams of blood shot through the air and fell over the sides of the fountain. Satan glanced around and saw that all of the fountains around the front of the temple spewed the same. People shrieked and backed away. Parents covered their children's eyes. One of the men stood tall, holding a huge cane high in the air.

"Listen all people!" he shouted, "You must not obey the man who comes to open the temple today. You must not listen to him."

Satan raised his arms summoning his armies. Suddenly he knew who they were. He had seen them before, but it had been a long time.

Obviously, it hadn't been long enough.

The prophet spoke, and although he had no microphone, his voice could be heard clearly.

"Your Messiah has already come. The man who comes to dedicate your temple is a charlatan."

Two huge men burst from the audience toward the bearded ones. They tried to grab their arms, but Elijah kept speaking as though he didn't even notice.

Several more people gathered around, holding their children, watching the blood squirt far and wide. Their thoughtful expressions worried Satan.

Enoch lifted his arms, and the blood changed back. The people were silent now, listening intently to the miracle workers.

Satan hurried forward. Somehow he had to stop them. He would kill them himself if he had to.

But he couldn't move. He stayed frozen in place, almost as if someone had bound his hands and feet.

They would pay. He had hurt them both once. And if it

took every ounce of his strength, he would complete the job he hadn't finished when they walked the earth.

* *

ANCIENT JEWS VALUED THE TESTIMONY OF WITNESSES. Jesus quoted the law in regard to using witnesses when there are accusations and troubles in a body of believers. In Matthew 18:16, He states, "But if he will not hear thee, then take with thee one or two more, that in the mouth of two or three witnesses every word may be established."

Newly commissioned by the Lord Himself, eleven of the disciples went on to be fearless witnesses—each one enduring hardship for the cause of Christ. Most met a martyr's death, but their fearless testimony was such a change from their former demeanor that it was further proof that the Lord had indeed risen from the dead.

Later, when thousands of Christians were tortured under Nero, a word for witness was coined, Martyr. For that is the ultimate witness.

In the throes of the torture of death, they stood firm. When I read accounts of these martyrs I am filled with awe. Who wouldn't be? Their lives were shining testimonies of Christ's power and grace.

Today the persecuted church in India, China, Muslim countries, and the former Soviet bloc has its own share of martyrs. The Bible says we are surrounded by a great cloud of witnesses charging us to run the race as well as they did.

And now, we look at the two greatest witnesses of all time.

- Two who dare to stand and fight the deepest evil.
- Two who minister in the most frightening time the world has ever known.
- Two who lead at least 144,000 to Christ, probably more.
- Two who fearlessly teach and preach.

• Two who are unable to be hurt until their time.

In the beginning of the Tribulation period there will come two who dare to stand. And many will stand with them.

LIVING FLAMES

No author except God Himself could write such thrilling narrative. Read now about these two witnesses.

> And there was given me a reed like unto a rod: and the angel stood, saying, Rise, and measure the temple of God, and the altar, and them that worship therein. But the court which is without the temple leave out, and measure it not; for it is given unto the Gentiles: and the holy city shall they tread under foot forty and two months. And I will give power unto my two witnesses, and they shall prophesy a thousand two hundred and threescore days, clothed in sackcloth. These are the two olive trees, and the two candlesticks standing before the God of the earth. And if any man will hurt them, fire proceedeth out of their mouth, and devoureth their enemies: and if any man will hurt them, he must in this manner be killed. These have power to shut heaven, that it rain not in the days of their prophecy: and have power over waters to turn them to blood, and to smite the earth with all plagues, as often as they will. And when they shall have finished their testimony, the beast that ascendeth out of the bottomless pit shall make war against them, and shall overcome them, and kill them. And their dead bodies shall lie in the street of the great city, which spiritually is called Sodom and Egypt, where also our Lord was crucified. And they of the people and kindreds and tongues and nations shall see their dead bodies three days and an half, and shall not suffer their dead bodies to be put in graves. And they that dwell upon the earth shall rejoice over

them, and make merry, and shall send gifts one to another; because these two prophets tormented them that dwelt on the earth. And after three days and an half the Spirit of life from God entered into them, and they stood upon their feet; and great fear fell upon them which saw them. And they heard a great voice from heaven saying unto them, Come up hither. And they ascended up to heaven in a cloud; and their enemies beheld them. And the same hour was there a great earthquake, and the tenth part of the city fell, and in the earthquake were slain of men seven thousand: and the remnant were affrighted, and gave glory to the God of heaven. The second woe is past; and, behold, the third woe cometh quickly. And the seventh angel sounded; and there were great voices in heaven, saying, The kingdoms of this world are become the kingdoms of our Lord, and of his Christ; and he shall reign for ever and ever. And the four and twenty elders, which sat before God on their seats, fell upon their faces, and worshipped God, Saying, We give thee thanks, O Lord God Almighty, which art, and wast, and art to come; because thou hast taken to thee thy great power, and hast reigned. And the nations were angry, and thy wrath is come, and the time of the dead, that they should be judged, and that thou shouldest give reward unto thy servants the prophets, and to the saints, and them that fear thy name, small and great; and shouldest destroy them which destroy the earth. And the temple of God was opened in heaven, and there was seen in his temple the ark of his testament: and there were lightnings, and voices, and thunderings, and an earthquake, and great hail (Rev. 11).

MYSTERY PROPHETS

In every prophecy book I researched, I found that the first question the author covered was who these men were. There are several different thoughts as to who they are, and I wish to remind you that most of what is out there is simply opinion. The Bible doesn't tell us for sure who these men are; so while we can look to other Scriptures and get a pretty good idea, we can't totally nail it down.

Most scholars agree on one of the witnesses: Elijah, that empowered prophet who was the only one about whom it is recorded that he called down fire from Heaven (2 Kings 1:10). Remember this is one of the miraculous abilities given to one of the witnesses. Revelation 11:5 reads, "And if any man will hurt them, fire proceedeth out of their mouth, and devoureth their enemies: and if any man will hurt them, he must in this manner be killed."

Because Elijah was able to do such an incredible miracle, the captains of Israel's armies feared him. In 2 Kings 1:13-14, one of the captains pleads for his life as a result of Elijah's power.

Don't forget as well that Elijah had the power to shut up the heavens and keep it from raining. 1 Kings 17:1 states, "And Elijah the Tishbite, who was of the inhabitants of Gilead, said unto Ahab, As the Lord God of Israel liveth, before whom I stand, there shall not be dew nor rain these years, but according to my word."

Of course, the main reason most scholars agree on the identity of Elijah is because this prophet didn't die. Rather he was caught up into Heaven in a chariot, a sign of the future Rapture of the church. 2 Kings 2:11-12 explains, "And it came to pass, as they still went on, and talked, that, behold, there appeared a chariot of fire, and horses of fire, and parted them both asunder; and Elijah went up by a whirlwind into heaven. And Elisha saw it, and he cried, My father, my father, the chariot of Israel, and the horsemen thereof. And he saw him no more: and he took hold of his own clothes, and rent them in two pieces."

The Bible states in Hebrews 9:27, "And as it is appointed unto men once to die, but after this the judgment." Since Elijah didn't die, then it could be assumed that he comes back later with a chance to be a true Superman proclaiming the message of the gospel during the most hideous of times.

Look again at Revelation 11:5-6, and see how the reasons stack up in favor of Elijah. "And if any man will hurt them, fire proceedeth out of their mouth, and devoureth their enemies: and if any man will hurt them, he must in this manner be killed. These have power to shut heaven, that it rain not in the days of their prophecy: and have power over waters to turn them to blood, and to smite the earth with all plagues, as often as they will."

1. The prophet Elijah had the power during his ministry to call down fire from Heaven.
2. Elijah had the power to put the earth in a drought.
3. Elijah didn't die; instead he was caught up to Heaven in a whirlwind.

Most scholars are divided on the identity of the other witness. Some feel the second witness is Moses. The reason for this is the reference to the water being turned to blood and the mention of plagues, which we know are events that seem to parallel what happened to Moses during his lifetime.

I believe the main problem with this is that Moses died a natural death. We know from Scripture that the Lord Himself buried Moses on Mount Nebo. Though the events mentioned here seem to indicate a Moses-like era of signs and wonders for the world's hardened hearts, from looking at Scripture I believe the other witness could be none other than Enoch.

Look at how Enoch ended his days on earth: Genesis 5:22-24 reads, "And Enoch walked with God after he begat Methuselah three hundred years, and begat sons and daughters: And all the days of Enoch were three hundred sixty and five years: And Enoch walked with God: and he was not; for God took him."

Enoch was taken up to Heaven, because he walked with God. I preached a sermon recently where I said that Enoch walked with God so closely that he walked all the way to

Heaven. I know that all of us as believers desire to have that kind of relationship with the Lord.

Enoch was taken up in a unique time frame. He was "gathered up" to Heaven just before the worldwide flood that destroyed the earth except for Noah and his family. This is an incredible picture of the rapture of the church. The Lord will gather His bride out of the earth before raining plagues, seals, and judgment upon it.

But whoever the witnesses are, we know one thing; God reveals them for a specific purpose and for a specific time. They again show God's mercy as they minister for three and a half years. They show God's amazing love for all people and their miraculous appearing, death, and resurrection will prove again to the world Who is really in charge.

In *Tribulation Force*, one of the books in the *Left Behind* series by Tim LaHaye and Jerry Jenkins, the authors imagine how a hostile encounter might happen to these witnesses during the tribulation period.

The two witnesses stopped preaching and stood shoulder to shoulder, glaring at the gunman as he approached. He ran full speed, firing as he ran, but the preachers stood rock solid, not speaking, not moving, arms crossed over their ragged robes. When the young man got to within five feet of them, he seemed to hit an invisible wall. He recoiled and flipped over backward, his weapon clattering away. His head smacked the ground first, and he lay groaning. Suddenly one of the preachers shouted, "You are forbidden to come nigh to the servants of the Most High God! We are under his protection until the due time, and woe to anyone who approaches without the covering of Yahweh himself." And as he finished, the other breathed from his mouth a column of fire that incinerated the man's clothes, consumed his flesh and organs, and in seconds left a charred skeleton smoking on the ground. The weapon melted and was fused to the cement, and the man's molten necklace dripped gold through the cavity in his chest.[1]

Perhaps this additional showing of mercy will help you and me to be merciful to those around us. Granted, we don't live in a world as terrible as the Tribulation time, but our world is sliding down the slippery slope of immorality and lewdness. During this time of debauchery, we need to stand up and be witnesses. We need to remember how much God loves everyone. He loved you and me while we were yet sinners. We need to recall His mercy on a daily basis. Then instead of becoming angry at that coworker who crosses us or family member who slights us, perhaps we will remember God's tremendous love for that individual. His great love is what brought us up out of the miry clay and compels us to continue showing and telling of His mercy to others. Why don't you take a moment right now and pray that God will help you become a great witness for Him?

DEATH ON CNN

After the recent war with Iraq, some critics said that since the American military couldn't capture Saddam Hussein and his sons immediately, that the war was a failed effort. They continued to insinuate that Iraq would become another Vietnam with no resolution and thousands of American deaths.

Then Odai and Qusai Hussein were killed. A few months later, their father was captured. This dynamic dramatically changed the world's perception of the war. If the two sons were killed, and the father was captured, the Iraqi people could finally relax and get on with their lives.

I was intrigued though by how the American military didn't immediately bury the sons' bodies, but allowed the whole world to see the pictures and videos. The top officials in the war knew Saddam's supporters would say the sons weren't really dead, that the United States government manufactured the news and the bodies for their own purposes.

So, the bodies were kept for several days where all the world would know and see for themselves that the wicked men were dead.

Steven R. Hurst of the Associated Press wrote this on August 3, 2003, in *The Salt Lake Tribune*,

> The Red Crescent acted as intermediary between Saddam's family and the U.S. military, which had kept the bodies in refrigerated storage at Baghdad International Airport. Military morticians had reconstructed the brothers' faces to look lifelike, and allowed Western journalists to videotape and photograph them, after Iraqi civilians voiced skepticism that Odai and Qusai were really dead. Images of the autopsied bodies were flashed across the Arab world by satellite broadcasters, largely dispelling lingering doubts.

Odai and Qusai deserved to die. Their deeds defy description. (Of course, they could have taken the mercy of God if they had simply believed.) But what amazed me was the fact that those men were not buried so the world would know they really were dead. All the news stations carried footage of them. All the newspapers carried their grisly photos.

Imagine the world's reaction if Saddam's sons suddenly stood up and walked out of the morgue. While on live TV, imagine the men standing in the streets of Baghdad and ascending up to Heaven.

Thankfully, Saddam's sons were buried. I have no desire for them to come back to life, but I brought up this example to show you what it will be like when the two witnesses lie in the streets of Jerusalem three and a half days and then are brought to life and then ascend to Heaven.

The Bible says they will do this with the world watching them. Even twenty years ago, it would be hard to imagine the world having the capability to watch such an event. But now it is not only possible but probable. Their resurrection and ascension will give more convincing proof that God is who He says He is. The lines will be drawn more clearly between God's way and Satan's way.

I believe the witnesses' resurrection and ascension will bring many people to Christ. It will probably have a cataclysmic effect on the Jewish people helping to bring the 144,000 to salvation and firing them up to evangelize the rest of the world.

SODOM AND EGYPT

Notice who kills the two witnesses. Satan himself. He is so furious over their "messing" with his plans, that he personally kills them both. This is supposed to be Satan's time to triumph — to spit in God's face. But yet, even as he kills the two witnesses, he is fulfilling prophecy. All people have to do is download Revelation 11 from the Internet to find out what happens next.

Consider that Jerusalem, being called Sodom and Egypt in this passage, tells us just how evil the world has become. We know from seeing how many Protestant churches are ordaining gay ministers and blessing same sex unions that our world is not only going toward that model right now but is in the midst of that model. Notice, too, that the people don't mourn when these witnesses are killed, but they celebrate the event as if it were Christmas. They give each other gifts and congratulate each other on getting rid of these men. It shows us the change from a culture that at one time condemned evil now not only embraces evil, it celebrates this great evil.

The time period of the witnesses' ministry is the same as our Lord's ministry when He was on the earth. Also think that these two witnesses will experience what our Lord went through. In the same city and the same amount of time before rising again. The parallels in Scripture are unbelievable. They don't happen by chance. Every jot and tittle of Scripture has a purpose.

When the two witnesses come back to life and ascend to Heaven, there is a great earthquake. A tenth of the city and 7,000 people are destroyed. Consider for a moment the great tragedy of September 11, 2001. In that catastrophic event, about 2,500 people were killed. Now consider that one earthquake wipes out 7,000. Do you see why so many people trust Christ during this time? How could they not?

Pastor Ray Stedman says, "One can easily imagine what a massive earthquake like that would do to modern Jerusalem, with its population of almost a million people. There is little doubt that this is literal since the largest earthquake fault on earth runs just east of Jerusalem, down the valley of the Jordan River. It is called the 'Great Rift Valley,' and it extends under the Dead Sea into Africa. It is the valley where the great African lakes, Lake Victoria, Lake Nyansa, and others are found. It is the line where the African continent butts up against Asia. We are familiar these days with the theory of continental drift and the movement of tectonic plates upon which the continents rest, so it is quite understandable that this would take place exactly as described."[2]

OVERWHELMING OIL

The witnesses have a final lesson for us. What gave them their power? What made them able to share with the world in such a commanding way the grace of the Lord Jesus Christ? Revelation 11:4 reads, "These are the two olive trees, and the two candlesticks standing before the God of the earth." Pastor Ray Stedman says, "It is easy to recognize the meaning of those symbols because Zechariah uses them as well."[3]

Look at Zechariah 4:1-6.

And the angel that talked with me came again, and waked me, as a man that is wakened out of his sleep, And said unto me, What seest thou? And I said, I have looked, and behold a candlestick all of gold, with a bowl upon the top of it, and his seven lamps

thereon, and seven pipes to the seven lamps, which
are upon the top thereof: And two olive trees by it,
one upon the right side of the bowl, and the other
upon the left side thereof. So I answered and spake
to the angel that talked with me, saying, What are
these, my lord? Then the angel that talked with me
answered and said unto me, Knowest thou not what
these be? And I said, No, my lord. Then he answered
and spake unto me, saying, This is the word of the
Lord unto Zerubbabel, saying, Not by might, nor by
power, but by my spirit, saith the Lord of hosts.

Paul declares that God will never leave the earth without
a witness. And indeed during the Great Tribulation He sends
two straight out of Old Testament times, dressed in the
traditional prophet's garb (sackcloth speaks of impending
judgment). This should also give us more proof that during
the Tribulation period, God is dealing again directly with
the Jew. Why else would He give them two of their ancient
prophets dressed in such a way that the Jews who know
the Scriptures won't be able to miss their presence or their
purpose? God gives them great power, which is symbolized
by the burning candlesticks and the olive trees.

If you have ever been to Israel, then you understand the
great importance of the olive to that land. For centuries they
have used the oil for ceremonial purposes, for nourishment,
for burning lamps, and a myriad of other uses. I remember
one of our Israeli guides picking up the small dish of olive
oil on the table and drinking it. He told me that almost all
Israelis drink a few teaspoons of oil a day—it is loved that
much.

"Not by might, nor by power but by my spirit saith the
Lord" is a favorite, oft-quoted passage by Christians today;
but if you place Zechariah's prophecy in the context of the
Great Tribulation you see what this passage is really talking
about. The reason the two witnesses are so effective is it
is obvious where they get their power. The oil represents

the Holy Spirit and His holy anointing on their work. They can't be killed until their work is done. They are the true Untouchables. No one can blow them out until God is ready for that to happen.

Revelation 11 describes the fear people feel as the witnesses come back to life. They understand that it is only God who can raise the dead. Remember what Jesus said in Matthew 10:28, "And fear not them which kill the body, but are not able to kill the soul: but rather fear him which is able to destroy both soul and body in hell." These witnesses understood that until their time came, they could not be harmed. Their holy anointing from the Spirit of God kept them safe and secure. Even their death is in the hand of God for in their resurrection many people see God's power. This event brings many to belief in Christ.

Prophecy scholar, the late John Walvoord wrote, "The resurrection of the two witnesses becomes an important testimony to the world at a time when the world was given to the worship of the world ruler and Satan seemed to be reigning supreme. Even though God was permitting the terrible events of the Great Tribulation to take place, including the catastrophes that will overtake most of the human race, it is also evident that God is still in control and can provide a ministry of testimony to the world even under these circumstances."[4] Walvoord's book used to belong to my late mother, Esther Burton. She loved the study of prophecy and had these words underlined. She obviously understood the great testimony and power of the witnesses.

Dear friend, doesn't that inspire you to serve the Lord in the here and now? You and I also have a holy anointing from the Spirit of God. We also have a mission. We also have people we need to be witnesses to. We know that He who began a good work in us will continue to perform it until the day of Jesus Christ.

Take a moment right now and thank God for His protection. Thank Him for His wondrous care and meticulous attention to every detail of your life.

Perhaps you might pray this prayer,

Lord, as I look at the two witnesses, I am inspired to be the same kind of witness for You. I desire to tell people around me of Your great love. I thank You for Your protection and for giving me the Holy Spirit to empower and protect me. Help me to live a life that pleases You. Help me to burn brightly in a dark world. In Your precious Son's name, Amen.

CHAPTER 11

The Battle

Megiddo, Israel
Revelation 16

THERE WAS NOTHING BUT BLOOD TO DRINK. Satan didn't need nourishment as those he commanded. Even his man of sin himself complained bitterly of thirst. Didn't these fools understand that they had to press on, to continue toward Megiddo? It was time. He was ready. This battle had been carefully scripted from the moment of his fall.

His armies had already feasted on the blood of those needless saints. Now they would taste blood all the time. With thousands of executions being performed daily, reality TV had taken on new dimensions with ratings going through the roof the gorier they were. The people had wanted to drink the blood of the saints; now let them drink blood all the time.

It was dark. Black almost. Everyone wore night-vision goggles as they came even now to the place where the Euphrates had once flowed.

The cosmic demons had risen from the pit, brandishing their unique brand of terror over the earth. They were locusts the size of dinosaurs with painted wings and long hair; orange, green, blue, they glowed. They accomplished much more than physical torment, they were able to sting the mind, accomplishing in minutes, years of torture. As they tortured, men and women came to battle God, their defenses down, swearing allegiance to the beast.

Now the armies gathered. All the powers in the world

waited. Nuclear bombs would go off in God's face.

And Satan would finally get what he wanted. Total rule. Total power.

He only had a few more moments to wait. He needed only to give the signal, and Hell would explode in the darkness.

Five. Four. Three.

He counted steadily.

Two.

His son had brought everything to a head, but now he must be destroyed to give his master what he really wanted. He had begged to live, and his begging made Satan sick.

Worthless chump.

In the end, Satan would rule.

One.

The explosion never came. Only deadly calm. Satan glanced up, surprised. Instead there was a huge roaring, an astounding light coming toward him in the darkness.

It could only be God.

Satan didn't see one of his men or his demons. He only saw the nail prints as Someone swooped down and picked him up like he was a pesky mosquito.

"Your power is gone." Satan heard the words but was helpless to do anything as he felt cords wrapping around his neck, his wrists, his legs.

He was going down into the pit.

He screamed, but no one could hear him.

* *

THROUGHOUT THE CENTURIES, PEOPLE HAVE SPOKEN AND WRITTEN MUCH ABOUT ARMAGEDDON. This battle will be fought at Megiddo, the most famous valley in the world. While standing there, it is easy to see why it made a good battlefield and why Satan will bring his armies to fight the final battle royal against God. Napoleon said of Megiddo, "All the armies of the world could maneuver here."

It is called the Valley of Jehoshaphat, ringed by the

Carmel Mountain Range. It is a fitting place for the last battle.

Only this is hardly a battle at all. Contrary to what's been portrayed in books and videos as "Armageddon," the real battle will be over in seconds.

There will be blood, but it will be the blood of the fated armies. The secret of this battle is that there really is no battle at all. When it comes down to it, Satan doesn't have a chance to shoot even the measliest arrow. God destroys the armies with a blink of His eye.

Throughout the years I've had many people ask me questions about prophecy and especially about Armageddon. The number one question is, "How will we fight with the Lord during the battle of Armageddon?" The truth is, my friend, we won't do the fighting. God doesn't have to fight either. God wins without a struggle. Why don't you read the text for yourself to find out why?

Revelation 16:17-21 explains,

> And the seventh angel poured out his vial into the air; and there came a great voice out of the temple of heaven, from the throne, saying, It is done. And there were voices, and thunders, and lightnings; and there was a great earthquake, such as was not since men were upon the earth, so mighty an earthquake, and so great. And the great city was divided into three parts, and the cities of the nations fell: and great Babylon came in remembrance before God, to give unto her the cup of the wine of the fierceness of his wrath. And every island fled away, and the mountains were not found. And there fell upon men a great hail out of heaven, every stone about the weight of a talent: and men blasphemed God because of the plague of the hail; for the plague thereof was exceeding great.

Revelation 19:11-20:6 goes on to say,

> And I saw heaven opened, and behold a white horse;

and he that sat upon him was called Faithful and True, and in righteousness he doth judge and make war. His eyes were as a flame of fire, and on his head were many crowns; and he had a name written, that no man knew, but he himself. And he was clothed with a vesture dipped in blood: and his name is called The Word of God. And the armies which were in heaven followed him upon white horses, clothed in fine linen, white and clean. And out of his mouth goeth a sharp sword, that with it he should smite the nations: and he shall rule them with a rod of iron: and he treadeth the winepress of the fierceness and wrath of Almighty God. And he hath on his vesture and on his thigh a name written, KING OF KINGS, AND LORD OF LORDS. And I saw an angel standing in the sun; and he cried with a loud voice, saying to all the fowls that fly in the midst of heaven, Come and gather yourselves together unto the supper of the great God; That ye may eat the flesh of kings, and the flesh of captains, and the flesh of mighty men, and the flesh of horses, and of them that sit on them, and the flesh of all men, both free and bond, both small and great. And I saw the beast, and the kings of the earth, and their armies, gathered together to make war against him that sat on the horse, and against his army. And the beast was taken, and with him the false prophet that wrought miracles before him, with which he deceived them that had received the mark of the beast, and them that worshipped his image. These both were cast alive into a lake of fire burning with brimstone. And the remnant were slain with the sword of him that sat upon the horse, which sword proceeded out of his mouth: and all the fowls were filled with their flesh. And I saw an angel come down from heaven, having the key of the bottomless pit and a great chain in his hand. And he laid hold on the dragon, that old serpent, which is the Devil, and Satan, and bound him a thousand years, And cast him into the bottomless pit, and shut him up, and set a seal upon him, that he should deceive the nations no more, till the thousand years should be fulfilled: and after that he must be loosed a little season. And I saw thrones, and they sat upon them, and judgment was given unto them: and I saw the souls of them that were beheaded for the witness of Jesus, and for the word of God, and which had not worshipped the beast, neither his image, neither had received his mark upon their foreheads, or in their hands; and they lived and reigned with Christ a thousand years. But the rest of the dead lived not again until the thousand years were finished. This is the first resurrection. Blessed and holy is he that hath part in the first resurrection: on such the second death hath no power, but they shall be priests of God and of Christ, and shall reign with him a thousand years.

THE JUDGMENTS

When you look through the judgments brought on the earth throughout the Tribulation period, you see how each judgment lessens the control of Satan, the Antichrist and the Beast. While they think they each are in control of the worldwide political, economical, and spiritual systems, each plague makes it harder and harder for them to maintain power. Let's look now at each of the judgments of the Great Tribulation Period and see how each brings the earth to the point of Armageddon.

Tim LaHaye writes, "This tired old planet has come under cruel times of famine, catastrophe, dictatorship, and many other causes of suffering. But the sixth chapter of Revelation introduces the most awesome period of time the world has ever known. This seven-year period decreed by God is for the primary purpose of shaking man loose from a false sense of security. Then he may call upon the name of the Lord before the end of the age."[1]

The Four Horsemen

The four horsemen represent world conditions. They show man's atrocity. They cause great suffering and hardship. Consider the world under such cruel dictators as Stalin, Hitler, Mussolini, and Hussein. The evils poured out on those under them cannot be fathomed. During the time under the Son of Satan, it will be worse. Let's look at the first seal, the rider on the White Horse.

Revelation 6:1-2 explains, "And I saw when the Lamb opened one of the seals, and I heard, as it were the noise of thunder, one of the four beasts saying, Come and see. And I saw, and behold a white horse: and he that sat on him had a bow; and a crown was given unto him: and he went forth conquering, and to conquer."

The Antichrist and the kingdom he rules ride this horse. His purpose is stated "conquering and to conquer." He has a bow in his hand, which is a symbol of aggressive warfare but notice that he holds no arrow. How does he conquer? By a false peace. He will promise to solve all the world's problems. What is given to him? A crown. That crown symbolizes his world dominance by his false peace.

The seal is the rider on the red horse. This is a symbol of war, because he has the ability to "take peace from the earth and that they should kill one another." As the Antichrist takes over the world, there are some nations who initially come into the world government only to revolt later thus bringing on a true World War III.

Revelation 6:5-6 says, "And when he had opened the third seal, I heard the third beast say, Come and see. And I beheld, and lo a black horse; and he that sat on him had a pair of balances in his hand. And I heard a voice in the midst of the four beasts say, A measure of wheat for a penny, and three measures of barley for a penny; and see thou hurt not the oil and the wine."

The black horse symbolizes famine. Since times of food deprivation often follow war, this horse shouldn't surprise us.

The next horse is the pale horse that means "corpselike." This horse signifies death. One fourth of the world's population will die as a result of the wars and famine.

The fifth seal is the martyred Tribulation saints. These are the believers who refused the mark of the beast. These are the saints who are saved as a direct result of the two witnesses and the ministry of the 144,000.

Revelation 6:9-11 explains, "And when he had opened the fifth seal, I saw under the altar the souls of them that were slain for the word of God, and for the testimony which they held: And they cried with a loud voice, saying, How long, O Lord, holy and true, dost thou not judge and avenge our blood on them that dwell on the earth? And white robes were given unto every one of them; and it was said unto them, that they should rest yet for a little season, until their fellowservants also and their brethren, that should be killed as they were, should be fulfilled."

Perhaps you've read the *Foxe's Book of Martyrs* and wondered at the great hardships the Christians written about endured. Maybe you've read of the persecution even now of believers all over the world. Nothing will compare to the persecution of the Tribulation saints. The comfort we can receive from this is that while the persecution is terrible and must be fulfilled, it is also "for a little season."

The sixth seal speaks of a great earthquake and how the sun becomes darkened and the moon turns to the color of red. These great catastrophes cause the world to recognize that this is the judgment of God because they have persecuted the Saints.

There are those scholars who teach that the church will be taken up in the middle of the Tribulation. They explain that the events occurring in the first half of the Tribulation period aren't that bad and so the church is taken then before the great "wrath" of the second half.

Do the things I've just described from the Word of God sound "easy" to you? Do they sound like they are nothing? Earthquakes, famine, darkness on the face of the earth, a world war, thousands getting killed, and great persecution for believers doesn't seem "easy" to me at all. These are just the beginning of sorrows.

THE TERRIBLE SILENCE

The reason for the silence in Heaven is almost too terrible to contemplate. It is the result of the revelation by Jesus Christ about what is going to happen on earth during the last half of the Tribulation.

The seventh seal represents the title deed to the earth. This seal begins the seven trumpet judgments. The horrible judgments cause the angels to hold their breath. Recently I saw a picture of an Israeli man who had just heard that his son had been killed in a suicide bombing. The expression on his face will haunt me forever. The man couldn't speak because of the awful news. In the same way, the terrible last half of the Tribulation will cause Heaven to take a collective half hour of silence.

The first angel takes a golden censer to make incense and "offer it with the prayers of all saints upon the golden altar." This is representative of the prayers of the saints under the altar in Revelation 6:9. The prayers for vengeance upon their enemies are about to be answered.

Remember, friend, our prayers are always heard by God. Even when you feel like your prayers are hitting the ceiling, understand by reading this verse that they are not. God hears every prayer you pray. While sometimes His answer might be "no" or "wait a while," He lovingly listens and remembers your concerns.

BLOW THE TRUMPET

Revelation 8:7 states, "The first angel sounded, and there followed hail and fire mingled with blood, and they were cast upon the earth: and the third part of trees was burnt up, and all green grass was burnt up."

The hail and fire fall on one third of the earth's surface

burning all the vegetation. Joel predicted this day as well in Joel 2:30-31.

Imagine millions of floating fish, whales, and mammals as the second trumpet sounds (Rev. 8:8-9). Then the third trumpet is a shining star that falls from Heaven causing the pollution of the world's water supply (Rev. 9:10-11). Then there is the fourth trumpet, where the day is reversed to night—there will be only eight hours of daylight and sixteen hours of darkness.

Next there is the warning angel who threatens (if this can be imagined) worse things to come. The fifth angel shows the judgment for the unsaved, the demons, and Satan himself.

Revelation 9:2-3 explains, "And he opened the bottomless pit; and there arose a smoke out of the pit, as the smoke of a great furnace; and the sun and the air were darkened by reason of the smoke of the pit. And there came out of the smoke locusts upon the earth: and unto them was given power, as the scorpions of the earth have power."

Once a year or so, when I drive to work, our church is almost totally clouded from view because of the fog. Some years it is worse than others. I remember one year when we first built on the property at Quentin Road, the fog was so thick I couldn't see the church from the road.

Imagine smoke and fog so thick that you can't see your own hand in front of your face. And this doesn't happen for one day or a week, but for weeks on end. Consider the worst smog of a Chicago, Los Angeles and New York combined and perhaps you can get just a glimpse of just how terrible this will be.

The creatures that torment men during this time have far more power than just the ability to hurt them physically. They are able to hurt mankind spiritually, persecuting with a vengeance.

These locusts on steroids will torment as the sting of the scorpion when it strikes. Though a scorpion's bite is seldom fatal, it is one of the most painful stings known. The venom causes extreme pain over a period of time. So the locust's torment will last five months.

I think the following verses are probably the saddest in Scripture. Revelation 9:6 reads, "And in those days shall men seek death, and shall not find it; and shall desire to die, and death shall flee from them."

I'm sure you can think back on a time you've had a stomach flu or food poisoning and felt so sick that you not only wished you could die, you hoped you wouldn't live. Consider a time when the physical and spiritual pain from these evil creatures will cause people to beg for death as a relief from their suffering.

In verse four of Revelation 9, we see how God protects those who have trusted Him during this time by not allowing the locusts to torment them.

Revelation 9:12 then reads, "One woe is past; and, behold, there come two woes more hereafter."

If the torment of these awful creatures wasn't enough, now there come two more. The sixth trumpet judgment is far worse for people, because the spirits are not only able to cause pain, but they can now kill.

Revelation 9:13-15 says, "And the sixth angel sounded, and I heard a voice from the four horns of the golden altar which is before God, Saying to the sixth angel which had the trumpet, Loose the four angels which are bound in the great river Euphrates. And the four angels were loosed, which were prepared for an hour, and a day, and a month, and a year, for to slay the third part of men."

These angels written of here are obviously fallen angels because of their bound state. They join with the terrible locust creatures in tormenting the earth.

Revelation 9:16 says, "And the number of the army of the horsemen were two hundred thousand thousand: and I heard the number of them." The four angels bound on the Euprates River seem to be leaders of these 200 million evil spirits. Already one fourth of the world's population has been killed, now these evil spirits kill another third.

PROTECTION FOR THE BELOVED

It is during this time that the Jewish people flee to the wilderness of Petra in Jordan where God protects them during the last three and a half years of the Tribulation. Revelation 12:6 explains, "And the woman fled into the wilderness, where she hath a place prepared of God, that they should feed her there a thousand two hundred and threescore days."

It is easy to see why Petra would be such an excellent hiding place for the Jews. There is only one narrow passage into the area, and the huge cliffs of rock have numerous caves and places to hide.

It is wonderful to see this picture of how God protects His remnant through the worst of His judgment. It is a future picture of how God is protecting His bride, the church, right now. In the midst of the worst moral conditions that have ever existed—in the terrible movies and television shows featuring homosexuality, promiscuity, adultery, and profanity—we see the church being protected by God. That's why it is so important that we as a body continue to stand fast in this dark world. Knowing we are protected, knowing God's hand is upon us, we press on: witnessing, sharing our light, giving of ourselves in everything we do.

Do you want to take a moment to reconfirm your commitment to be the light God wants you to be? He has promised to protect you just as He will protect His people during the Tribulation. Why don't you take that step of faith right now?

THE GREAT TRIBULATION

The second three and a half years bring even more catastrophe upon the earth. We know that already a third of the sea has turned to blood during the second trumpet. This second judgment includes the entire sea.

During a recent electrical blackout in cities in the United States and Canada, there was much talk about how people should boil the water before they drank it. Consider how it would be if all the oceans turned into thick, disgusting blood, killing all the life inside them. People will panic as they search for clean drinking water. Even Hinckley and Schmidt or any water company, will be unable to find adequate water. The only water available will be water that is already stored. Think about how people react when they don't have electricity which isn't even necessary for sustaining life. People will be willing to kill for a drink.

You can see how this judgment, almost more than any of the others, makes it impossible for man to rely on his own resources. The greatest minds in the world won't be able to solve this problem. People will have to cry out to God, which of course, is the purpose for this judgment.

Revelation 16:8-9 says, "And the fourth angel poured out his vial upon the sun; and power was given unto him to scorch men with fire. And men were scorched with great heat, and blasphemed the name of God, which hath power over these plagues: and they repented not to give him glory."

When you wake up every morning, are you surprised that the sun has risen? When you walk outside in the evening, are you surprised to see the sun set? Of course you aren't. You expect the sun to rise and set. You probably don't give it much thought. Imagine what will happen when a third of the sun is darkened but what remains scorches the earth with a terrible heat. This will be global warming's worst nightmare! The conditions will already be terrible. There is barely any water and now men and women are infernally hot, so hot they again wish they could get away from the intense heat. They will get their wish.

The next judgment is darkness. Following the great heat wave, far greater than any that have happened in our world, there will be a time of darkness. This is another expression of God's mercy in the midst of His judgment. While mankind cries out in pain, God gives them relief from the sun.

This judgment seems to center on the throne of the Son of Satan. Revelation 16:10 states, "And the fifth angel poured out his vial upon the seat of the beast; and his kingdom was full of darkness; and they gnawed their tongues for pain." The darkness seems to emanate from the Antichrist's throne. This darkness will prevail for some time. As you read Revelation 16, take note of verse 11, "And blasphemed the God of heaven because of their pains and their sores, and repented not of their deeds." While men and women seem to understand that these judgments are from God, many turn away from His mercy. They blaspheme God, when they could simply accept the gift of God's Son.

Tim LaHaye writes, in light of this passage, "Let it be understood that when men reject the Lord, it is not because of philosophical doubts of unexplained answers to unanswered questions, but hardness of heart and love for sin."[2]

It shows us again the wickedness of our own hearts, and how no matter how clear it is that God is God, some men and women will still reject Him.

The sixth bowl judgment written of in Revelation 16:12-16 comes in two parts. First the River Euprates dries up which is a preparation for the "battle of the great day of God Almighty" or the "day of the Lord." Then the massive demon forces bring the forces of the world to the Valley of Megiddo for the great battle of Armageddon.

Consider what it would be like to be someone who got saved during the Tribulation. If you managed to make it through to the end of the seven years, you would be waiting for one thing and one thing only—the drying up of the Euphrates River. You knew that if you could just hang on to that point, God would come, bringing His armies to destroy the powers of darkness.

You would hover close to the radio, waiting, listening. You would try to watch the news for any sign, though it would be difficult to watch all the terrible things happening around you.

When the river dried up, you would experience deliverance.

In the blink of an eye, Satan, his myriad of evil armies,

all the forces of men and women who tried to go against God, will be destroyed. The blood is to the horse's bridle, but it isn't the blood of God's armies.

At that moment, the battle is over.

Satan will be bound for 1,000 years.

Christ will rule and reign.

It will be a glorious time.

But there is one battle still to come.

CHAPTER 12

The Last Battle

The Bottomless Pit
Revelation 20

THE DULL ROARING REMINDED HIM OF WHEN HE FIRST FELL. He hadn't moved for what seemed like an eternity. The darkness seemed to have no end. He could see nothing, hear nothing. The vast emptiness of it all only served to remind him of his status.

He had gathered every available force, every available man and woman, every spirit being, every weapon he had ever induced man to make.

He remembered looking out across the valley at the armies, more than even his eye could see. Their combined hatred and ferocity mollified his spirit somehow. Together they would fight.

And they would battle with the same hatred he had possessed since eternity past. He knew they would for he had empowered them. He saw his son sitting on a black stallion, poised, powerful, his hair falling across his forehead. His fist clenched toward the Heavens. All the armies bowed to him, ready to lay their lives down in service to their leader.

Satan had decided he would kill his son just as the battle began, and then he would take his rightful place in the front of all. He was tired of those who still worshipped the beast. He had thought he would be content working through this leader, but he had found that he wanted the total adoration, the spiritual fervor that position brought.

He started to raise his hands, signaling the deepest evil

when the roaring suddenly increased. A light brighter than the sun burst through the clouds. It happened so fast that it seemed it had always been.

He saw blood oozing out of the horses and his men, filling up the valley, spilling over the sides.

Before he could move, cords wrapped around the very essence of his being. Then he felt the darkness closing around him and he could see and hear nothing.

Only this nagging voice telling him that he had lost.

That was the worst torment of all.

He hadn't seen anything but darkness for so long that he wondered what that small pin prick was at first.

It looked like light.

Then he heard something. A glorious sound. Anything was better than all this darkness, this nothingness.

Before he could think, a terrible angel stood in front of him.

Satan recognized him as the Captain of God's Angels.

His eyes flashed fire. His golden robe blinded him.

He heard a clank, then a groan, as the shuddering cords fell off his being.

"For a little season," the Captain said, "you are released."

He couldn't get out of the pit fast enough.

He knew the thousand years must be up. But there would still be some idiots who would follow him.

Even without his influence, man's heart held the deepest evil.

With a shudder he swept toward the earth.

This last battle was revenge.

* *

THINK ABOUT WHAT WOULD HAPPEN IF SATAN AND HIS DEMONS WERE TAKEN OUT OF THE PICTURE FOR YOU AS A BELIEVER. Spiritual warfare would cease. There would be no more spiritual wickedness in high places. Now remove yourself to a world unlike the one in which you are now living. Oh, it may look somewhat the same with grass, trees, flowers, buildings, homes, but it will look far more beautiful, so lovely in fact that it will make the world you once lived in seem like a mere shadow of this one.

The King of that world rules with a rod of iron, so there is hardly a need for a police force. Huge predators no longer need to eat each other, so you can sleep in even the most remote village in perfect safety. Food is lush and abundant, pollution is nonexistent, thanks to the perfect environment, and people live for hundreds of years so death is something that almost never happens. There is no longer any worldly temptation, no Hollywood, no porn shops, no indecent billboards, nothing to make the wicked flesh leap.

Only perfect beauty. The Kingdom for which every believer longs is here.

But even in the absence of worldly temptation and Satan's evil presence, the pull of man's flesh is so strong that when Satan is loosed for a short season, there are many who follow his evil leadership.

There have been many people throughout the years who have said to me, "Pastor, I don't understand why Satan is loosed for this time after the Millennium. Why doesn't God just go ahead and cast him into Hell?"

I don't think any pastor or commentator totally understands why God does this, but I do know one thing. This scenario described in Revelation 20 does away with the argument that man's environment is what causes him to do evil. It shuts down the notion that man doesn't know any better and is simply a victim to external forces beyond his control. Or that every man doesn't have a chance to be saved.

I think this brief period that Satan is loosed shows once and for all the truth Jeremiah wrote, "The heart is deceitful above all things, and desperately wicked: who can know it" (Jer. 17:9).

Who can comprehend this wickedness? Who can

understand how Satan's absence brings about the last battle? We can only look to our Father and confess our own sins. We can only say with the Psalmist, "Search me, O God, and know my heart: try me, and know my thoughts: And see if there be any wicked way in me, and lead me in the way everlasting" (Ps. 139:23).

Our great God wants to change us into His image. He wants us to be like His dear Son. He can only do that if we continue to mortify our flesh and walk in the Spirit of God. We can only do that through His unfailing strength. I know studying about Satan and his devious plans has caused me to be more aware of God's awesome power. And I also know that seeing how some people are still willing to be deceived even during a time of light, causes me to fall on my face before my righteous God. I know this has helped me to continue to rely on God's grace to get me through each day.

Has this study also helped you to see the wicked pull of your own heart? Maybe you've endured a recent rebuke by a supervisor or a peer, and you have been harboring thoughts of resentment toward that person. It could be that you have felt frustrated at someone else moving up the career ladder faster than you are. Perhaps you've seen a weakness in your children that you see also in yourself. Whatever the case, I would like to encourage you to take this opportunity to fall on your knees before the Lord and confess your sin. Rely only on His mercy to renew and strengthen you for the task ahead. He has promised to forgive in the verse, "If we confess our sins, he is faithful and just to forgive us our sins, and to cleanse us from all unrighteousness" (1 John 1:9). Cling to that promise right now, and see how God will work through you in the future.

The First Resurrection

Look now at the events immediately following the Battle of Armageddon.

Revelation 20:4-6 states,

And I saw thrones, and they sat upon them, and judgment was given unto them: and I saw the souls of them that were beheaded for the witness of Jesus, and for the word of God, and which had not worshipped the beast, neither his image, neither had received his mark upon their foreheads, or in their hands; and they lived and reigned with Christ a thousand years. But the rest of the dead lived not again until the thousand years were finished. This is the first resurrection. Blessed and holy is he that hath part in the first resurrection: on such the second death hath no power, but they shall be priests of God and of Christ, and shall reign with him a thousand years.

Remember, there are two phases to Christ's resurrection. As Dave Hunt said once when he spoke at our church, "Just as when you first drive toward the mountains, it looks like one big mountain until you drive closer to see more distinct peaks, so after Christ's coming, the New Testament writers saw His second coming as two distinct phases." First there is the Rapture of the Church, the great catalyst that helps bring on the seven year Tribulation. During the Battle of Armageddon or just before the Millennium, the Son of Satan and the False Prophet are killed and await the Great White Throne Judgment. Satan is also bound during this time. After the Tribulation, during the Battle of Armageddon, Christ appears with His saints (you and me).

During the glorious appearing, the Old Testament saints and the Tribulation saints will appear along with the Church Age saints. This is called the First Resurrection. This is a happy resurrection, because as we saw in verse six, the second death has no power over this resurrection. The second death is when all those who haven't trusted Christ as Savior are thrown into the lake of fire.

If you have trusted Christ as your Savior, then you too will be happy during this resurrection. You can be assured that you will be an active participant during this time.

Recently, I read an article about the men of the Bataan Death March—which led to the deaths of two-thirds of the 12,000 Americans trapped in the Philippines after Pearl Harbor. A local school, Maywood Proviso East High School, developed a website that detailed these heroic men. Many of the men in the 192nd division, originally organized as the 33rd Tank Company came from Maywood, Ill. Ten days after Pearl Harbor, U.S. forces in the Philippines fell back on the Bataan peninsula and were trapped there, forced to surrender and made to march through jungles with little food or water to the first of several camps where they provided slave labor. Many men died later in the war when they were sent to Japan in unmarked ships that were sunk by U.S. and British submarines. This website chronicles the individual stories of nearly 200 men.[1] Not surprisingly, the students' project won the 2003-2004 Illinois State Board of Education team award for educational excellence.

The survivors of that terrible march are now in their 80's. Consider for a moment their feelings as they returned home after the war. Only 4,000 of the original 12,000 POW's walked out of the camps after World War II. Most looked like skeletons after years of starvation and maltreatment. After having seen so many people die, they certainly had to feel unbelievably fortunate not to have died. They must have felt and still feel as though they had been snatched from the jaws of death.

This could be a small taste of how we will feel as we participate in the first resurrection. We will know for certain that because we are there, we will not be cast into Hell as those in the second resurrection that is unto death. We will feel a gratefulness and joy far beyond anything we could understand now.

1,000 YEARS OF BLISS

Revelation 20:6 states, "Blessed and holy is he that hath part in the first resurrection: on such the second death hath no power, but they shall be priests of God and of Christ, and shall reign with him a thousand years."

Clarence Larkin, in his book, gives five reasons for accepting the pre-millennial view of the Lord's return. These relate directly to Revelation 20 which states that the Millennial period is a thousand years long.

1. When Christ comes [the Second Coming] He will raise the dead, but the Righteous dead are to be raised before the Millennium, that they may reign with Christ during the thousand years, hence there can be no Millennium before Christ comes (Rev. 20:5).
2. When Christ comes Satan shall be bound, but as Satan is to be bound during the Millennium, there can be no Millennium until Christ comes (Rev. 20:1-3).
3. When Christ comes Antichrist is to be destroyed, but as Antichrist is to be destroyed before the Millennium there can be no Millennium until Christ comes (2 Thes. 2:8; Rev. 19:20).
4. When Christ comes the Jews are to be restored to their own land but as they are to be restored to their own land before the Millennium there can be no Millennium until Christ comes (Ezekiel 36:34-38; Rev. 1:7; Zech. 12:10).
5. When Christ comes it will be unexpectedly, and we are commanded to watch lest He take us unawares. Now if He is not coming until after the Millennium, and the Millennium is not yet here, why command us to watch for an event that is over a thousand years off?[2]

A literal view of prophetic events leaves the student with no doubt that Christ's coming is before the Millennium. This wonderful time is mentioned many times in Scripture. There are hundreds of verses in the Bible that predict an earthly kingdom where Jesus Christ rules and reigns. If you read through the Major and Minor Prophets, you see how this was a source of encouragement to the faithful remnant of Israel. The message is clear. No matter how bad things are, no matter how bleak your situation, one day God's Kingdom will fill the earth and true righteousness will be the standard for all people.

Earlier I wrote of Daniel's interpretation of Nebuchadnezzar's vision. He wrote of the Millennial time in Daniel 2:34-35, "Thou sawest till that a stone was cut out without hands, which smote the image upon his feet that were of iron and clay, and brake them to pieces. Then was the iron, the clay, the brass, the silver, and the gold, broken to pieces together, and became like the chaff of the summer threshing floors; and the wind carried them away, that no place was found for them: and the stone that smote the image became a great mountain, and filled the whole earth."

All the kingdoms of the world are no match for God's Kingdom. During the Tribulation period, this stone cut without hands destroys the last earthly kingdom represented by the ten toes. Can you imagine a more perfect image of God's power and might? A stone cut without hands. Just as the Jewish people were to use uncut stones to build their altars, so this final Stone will destroy the existing kingdom and establish a Kingdom so wonderful and awesome that it fills the whole earth.

THE RULING CITY

Zechariah 14:8-21 speaks of the importance of Jerusalem during the Tribulation and then during the Millennium.

And it shall be in that day, that living waters shall go out from Jerusalem; half of them toward the former sea, and half of them toward the hinder sea: in summer and in winter shall it be. And the Lord shall be king over all the earth: in that day shall there be one Lord, and his name one. All the land shall be turned as a plain from Geba to Rimmon south of Jerusalem: and it shall be lifted up, and inhabited in her place, from Benjamin's gate unto the place of the first gate, unto the corner gate, and from the tower of Hananeel unto the king's winepresses. And men shall dwell in it, and there shall be no more utter destruction; but Jerusalem shall be safely inhabited. And this shall be the plague wherewith the Lord will smite all the people that have fought against Jerusalem; Their flesh shall consume away while they stand upon their feet, and their eyes shall consume away in their holes, and their tongue shall consume away in their mouth. And it shall come to pass in that day, that a great tumult from the Lord shall be among them; and they shall lay hold every one on the hand of his neighbour, and his hand shall rise up against the hand of his neighbour. And Judah also shall fight at Jerusalem; and the wealth of all the heathen round about shall be gathered together, gold, and silver, and apparel, in great abundance. And so shall be the plague of the horse, of the mule, of the camel, and of the ass, and of all the beasts that shall be in these tents, as this plague. And it shall come to pass, that every one that is left of all the nations which came against Jerusalem shall even go up from year to year to worship the King, the Lord of hosts, and to keep the feast of tabernacles. And it shall be, that whoso will not come up of all the families of the earth unto Jerusalem to worship the King, the Lord of hosts, even upon them shall be no rain. And if the family of Egypt go not up, and come not, that have no rain; there shall be the plague, wherewith the Lord will smite the heathen that come not up to keep the feast of tabernacles. This shall be the punishment of Egypt, and the punishment of all nations that come not up to keep the feast of tabernacles. In that day shall there be upon the bells of the horses, HOLINESS UNTO THE LORD; and the pots in the Lord's house shall be like the bowls before the altar. Yea, every pot in Jerusalem and in Judah shall be holiness unto the Lord of hosts: and all they that sacrifice shall come and take of them, and seethe therein: and in that day there shall be no more the Canaanite in the house of the Lord of hosts.

The world may not want to accept right now that
Jerusalem is even part of Israel, but there is coming a day
when Jerusalem will be the center of the world. All people
will come to Jerusalem to worship the king. This will be
a true kingdom of holiness. Those who disobey will be
immediately punished. The standards won't be those of men
but of God.

Isaiah 2:2-4 reads,

> And it shall come to pass in the last days, that the
> mountain of the Lord's house shall be established in
> the top of the mountains, and shall be exalted above
> the hills; and all nations shall flow unto it. And many
> people shall go and say, Come ye, and let us go up to
> the mountain of the Lord, to the house of the God of
> Jacob; and he will teach us of his ways, and we will
> walk in his paths: for out of Zion shall go forth the
> law, and the word of the Lord from Jerusalem. And
> he shall judge among the nations, and shall rebuke
> many people: and they shall beat their swords into
> plowshares, and their spears into pruning hooks:
> nation shall not lift up sword against nation, neither
> shall they learn war any more.

What will we as believers be doing during the
Millennium? Our verse in Revelation stated that we would
be reigning with Christ during that thousand years. Isn't
that exciting? We get to watch and participate during the
wonderful time of the Millennium. We witness peace on
earth established. We get to see animals lying peacefully
beside each other. Isaiah 11:6 explains, "The wolf also shall
dwell with the lamb, and the leopard shall lie down with the
kid; and the calf and the young lion and the fatling together;
and a little child shall lead them." We get to see the earth
work in glorious harmony just as it was meant to be. We will
get to see the world truly experience peace.

I believe the Millennium shows us that this earth is important to God. He will be the One who eventually saves it. We shouldn't worry about every environmentalist saying we need to save the world. This doesn't mean I feel we should waste things and hurt the environment, but this should help the believer keep in mind that only God can save the earth, and during this time He will.

Also the Millennium shows us that God always keeps His Word. He promised Israel many times in Scripture coming world peace where Jerusalem is the capital of the world. During this thousand years, Israel experiences a utopia far beyond even their wildest dreams.

Isaiah 65:17-25 tells us even more,

> For, behold, I create new heavens and a new earth: and the former shall not be remembered, nor come into mind. But be ye glad and rejoice for ever in that which I create: for, behold, I create Jerusalem a rejoicing, and her people a joy. And I will rejoice in Jerusalem, and joy in my people: and the voice of weeping shall be no more heard in her, nor the voice of crying. There shall be no more thence an infant of days, nor an old man that hath not filled his days: for the child shall die an hundred years old; but the sinner being an hundred years old shall be accursed. And they shall build houses, and inhabit them; and they shall plant vineyards, and eat the fruit of them. They shall not build, and another inhabit; they shall not plant, and another eat: for as the days of a tree are the days of my people, and mine elect shall long enjoy the work of their hands. They shall not labour in vain, nor bring forth for trouble; for they are the seed of the blessed of the Lord, and their offspring with them. And it shall come to pass, that before they call, I will answer; and while they are yet speaking, I will hear. The wolf and the lamb shall feed together, and the lion shall eat straw like the bullock: and dust

shall be the serpent's meat. They shall not hurt nor destroy in all my holy mountain, saith the Lord.

A LITTLE SEASON

Remember, Satan was bound, not destroyed, before the Millennium started. We've already looked at the Scripture that showed Satan will be loosed for a little season.

Revelation 20:7-10 explains, "And when the thousand years are expired, Satan shall be loosed out of his prison, And shall go out to deceive the nations which are in the four quarters of the earth, Gog and Magog, to gather them together to battle: the number of whom is as the sand of the sea. And they went up on the breadth of the earth, and compassed the camp of the saints about, and the beloved city: and fire came down from God out of heaven, and devoured them. And the devil that deceived them was cast into the lake of fire and brimstone, where the beast and the false prophet are, and shall be tormented day and night for ever and ever."

Some people have read here when it says that those who battle God at this point are "as the sand of the sea," and they are amazed. How could there be that many people reject God after a time of perfect peace and order? How could there be people that, despite perfect light, reject God and all that He is?

Once again we must remember the depravity of the human heart. Why are there so many people who go against God in the real last battle? Because during this time of perfect peace and prosperity, the life span of man will be increased. Scripture tells us that a man or woman will be considered a child until he or she is 100 years old. Can you imagine the number of children that will be born during this time? No war. Perfect economic stability. No tornadoes, hurricanes, earthquakes or anything else that might affect the population. Can you imagine a more ideal environment in which to raise children? I know when I was in Bible College and before I married, I worried about bringing children into this wicked world. During the Millennium, this won't be a worry.

Humanism teaches that man can change if simply his environment changes. That in himself he has the capability to become a better person. This final battle instigated by Satan douses that theory. Even in the absence of worldly temptation and the devil, man is still capable of rebellion against God.

Today, we as believers are capable of rebellion against God. Every day we need to guard against this tendency. Remember, the Holy Spirit leads us like a dove, not like an elephant! We need to keep our hearts open and tender before Him, asking the Lord to show us our wickedness and relying on our Father for strength. Otherwise, we aren't going to receive rewards in Heaven and even more importantly, our rebellion might keep other people from trusting Christ as Savior.

THE GREAT WHITE THRONE

The most chilling words in the Bible concern the Great White Throne Judgment. Revelation 20:11-15 explains,

> And I saw a great white throne, and him that sat on it, from whose face the earth and the heaven fled away; and there was found no place for them. And I saw the dead, small and great, stand before God; and the books were opened: and another book was opened, which is the book of life: and the dead were judged out of those things which were written in the books, according to their works. And the sea gave up the dead which were in it; and death and hell delivered up the dead which were in them: and they were judged every man according to their works. And death and hell were cast into the lake of fire. This is the second death. And whosoever was not found written in the book of life was cast into the lake of fire.

Understand this, dear ones. While you read this passage and tremble, understand this passage is not written for the believer. The Great White Throne Judgment is for unbelievers. Before this point, just after the battle of Gog and Magog, the Devil is cast into Hell. We can see from the part of the passage that the Antichrist and the False Prophet will have already been thrown in Hell before the Millennium, and they will have been tormented for the entire thousand years. This should put to rest any theory set forth that Hell is simply annihilation. It is real, it is burning with fire and brimstone, it is anguish and man is obviously capable of continuing to be tormented forever.

Who are the dead, small and great who stand before God? These are those who are dead in trespasses and sins because of their rejection of Jesus Christ. Notice also that it doesn't matter to God whether you are "small," meaning you haven't achieved worldly success or stature, or "great," meaning you have achieved worldly success. To God all that matters is whether you have accepted His Son. All those at this judgment haven't done that.

These will be judged by the cold, unbending Law. This passage also indicates that there will be degrees of Hell as the dead are judged from books of their works. This doesn't mean that any of these works will merit Heaven or eternity with God. It means that the deeds will determine their degree of penalty, though all will be punished. I believe all of us would agree that someone like Saddam Hussein would deserve a greater punishment than someone who never murdered. Understand this, however: every person at this judgment is doomed to eternal torment. Ecclesiastes 12:14 says, "For God shall bring every work into judgment, with every secret thing, whether it be good, or whether it be evil."

Imagine the horror at realizing that your name is not written in the Lamb's Book of Life at this judgment. Especially when Jesus Christ Himself paid the sin debt of every person in the world. Especially when going to Heaven had been a matter of simple belief and trust in the finished work of Christ at Calvary.

Studying the Great White Throne causes me to want to tell the good news of Jesus Christ to every person I know. This is what motivates me every time I speak on television or radio. Sometimes when I stand in the pulpit, my heart constricts as I think about the Great White Throne. Considering this final judgment gives impetus to my every action, so that I can be the most effective witness that I can be for my Lord. I certainly don't want any of my friends, family, neighbors or even people I don't know to take part in that judgment. I desire for them to take part in the first resurrection—and that responsibility rests with me.

I know you must desire the same, or you wouldn't be reading this book. Can I take a moment right now to encourage you to find ways to give out the gospel to your friends and loved ones? Is there someone who needs to hear about Jesus? The shyest person in my church faithfully gives out tracts that tell of the plan of salvation. She knows that while she would probably rather die than speak to someone she doesn't know about the Lord, she can give out a tract. We can do no less. Would you take on this burden of soul winning? Will you work with Christians around the world to keep people from being cast into Hell forever?

It is our greatest mission. We must fulfill it.

NEW HEAVEN AND EARTH

God always leaves us with a promise. Although Satan is a terrible being who is bent on destroying God, in the last two chapters of Revelation we see that Satan was only a tiny tool in a great master plan.

Revelation 21:1-8 says,

> And I saw a new heaven and a new earth: for the first heaven and the first earth were passed away; and there was no more sea. And I John saw the holy city, new Jerusalem, coming down from God out of heaven, prepared as a bride adorned for her husband. And I heard a great voice out of heaven saying, Behold, the

tabernacle of God is with men, and he will dwell with them, and they shall be his people, and God himself shall be with them, and be their God. And God shall wipe away all tears from their eyes; and there shall be no more death, neither sorrow, nor crying, neither shall there be any more pain: for the former things are passed away. And he that sat upon the throne said, Behold, I make all things new. And he said unto me, Write: for these words are true and faithful. And he said unto me, It is done. I am Alpha and Omega, the beginning and the end. I will give unto him that is athirst of the fountain of the water of life freely. He that overcometh shall inherit all things; and I will be his God, and he shall be my son. But the fearful, and unbelieving, and the abominable, and murderers, and whoremongers, and sorcerers, and idolaters, and all liars, shall have their part in the lake which burneth with fire and brimstone: which is the second death.

If you get a chance today, read the last two chapters of Revelation. It is amazing to read of God's faithfulness and His great love for us. This new Heaven and earth will be far better than any earth this world has ever known, even better than before the flood and the days in the Garden of Eden.

In this passage, we read that God gives to all that thirst the water of life freely. The choice is up to us. The choice is up to every person in the world today. We can accept this water of life now and never thirst spiritually again, or we can reject Him and burn eternally in the Lake of Fire.

In C. S. Lewis' *The Chronicles of Narnia*, the characters that have lived in Narnia have completed their time and work there. In a closing chapter titled "Further Up and Further In," Aslan, the lion who represents Christ, has come to take them home. They are headed away from Narnia and are about to enter Aslan's land. But they are met with familiar scenes. One of the characters cries out: "I have come home at last! This is my real country! I belong here. This is the land I have been looking for all my life, though I never knew it till now. The reason why we loved the old Narnia is that it sometimes looked a little like this."

When my granddaughter Amanda listened to a tape of that story when she was 4 years old she said, "That's Heaven, right? That's where Aslan is taking everybody—to Heaven."

While I don't agree with all of Lewis' views on Heaven, I do know that when we get there, Amanda will say along with all of us, "This is the land I've been looking for my whole life, though I never knew it until now."

Dear friend, you too are looking for a land that is brighter than day. I've been so blessed by this study of the Son of Satan. I've continually been amazed at the wonderful detail of God's plan for the ages. Although the earth passes through a time of economic prosperity at the beginning of the Tribulation, there is soon a horrifying realization that God is judging the earth. But the judgments are what give people who are willing to trust Christ, reason to do so.

We have seen over and over again that in the midst of the most horrifying judgment, resides God's great mercy. The events of the end time inspire me in my walk with Christ. I want to draw closer and closer to Him. I want to share His glorious message of eternal water with all who will listen. I desire to bring glory and honor to Him because He is not only the ruler, but the over-ruler as well.

My prayer is that these desires are yours as well. My concern is that you continue to serve our Lord Jesus Christ. I hope we will both hear from our Savior's lips, "Well done, thou good and faithful servant."

Even so, come Lord Jesus!

For more information about how to go to Heaven, for help in living the Christian life, and/or to receive a free prophecy chart, use the enclosed postage-paid card or write to

Dr. James A. Scudder
Victory In Grace
60 Quentin Road
Lake Zurich, IL 60047
1-800-78-GRACE (1-800-784-7223)
You can also visit us online at www.victoryingrace.org

For questions about this book or to watch a video message from Dr. Scudder, visit the website at www.sonofsatan.org

HOW TO KNOW FOR SURE YOU ARE GOING TO HEAVEN

REALIZE FIRST THAT EVERYONE IS LESS PERFECT THAN A HOLY GOD. WE ARE ALL SINNERS AND UNABLE TO SAVE OURSELVES.

"For all have sinned, and come short of the glory of God" (Rom. 3:23).

God says that even our good deeds are unclean in his sight. Our good deeds can never pay the price for our sin.

"But we are all as an unclean thing, and all our righteousnesses are as filthy rags; and we all do fade as a leaf; and our iniquities, like the wind, have taken us away" (Isa. 64:6).

THE RESULT AND PENALTY OF SIN IS DEATH, WHICH MEANS SEPARATION FROM GOD FOREVER.

"For the wages of sin is death; but the gift of God is eternal life through Jesus Christ our Lord" (Rom. 6:23).

Because we have sinned, we all deserve to be separated from God forever. God hates sin because it separates us from Him but He loves us, the sinner.

Heaven is a perfect place; therefore no sin can enter there. Man must be perfect to gain entrance.

"And there shall in no wise enter into it any thing that defileth, neither whatsoever worketh abomination, or maketh a lie: but they which are written in the Lamb's book of life" (Rev. 21:27).

Nothing man can do could help obtain the perfection God requires for Heaven.

> "For by grace are ye saved through faith; and that not of yourselves: it is the gift of God: Not of works, lest any man should boast" (Eph. 2:8-9).

> Salvation is only by God's grace. Grace means unmerited favor or undeserved mercy. A gift is not earned or paid for or it would not be a gift.

> "But to him that worketh not, but believeth on him that justifieth the ungodly, his faith is counted for righteousness" (Rom. 4:5).

Christ made a complete payment for all sin and offers His righteousness to us.

> "For he hath made him to be sin for us, who knew no sin; that we might be made the righteousness of God in him" (2 Cor. 5:21).

> We have seen that we are all sinners and that the penalty of sin is eternal separation from God. We have also seen that God loves us and offers us the gift of eternal life. He requires only our belief, our trust in that payment.

> How could a holy God give eternal life to sinners? Only through His Son who died on the cross to make a full payment for all sin.

All we have to do to have eternal life is believe in Jesus Christ.

> "For God so loved the world, that he gave his only begotten Son, that whosoever believeth in him should not perish, but have everlasting life" (John 3:16).

This verse does not say anything about promising God good works in order to be saved. It doesn't mention joining a church or being baptized or even quitting all your sinning. The word believe means to trust, depend, or rely upon.

Will you place your trust in Jesus Christ to save your soul? To trust Him means to rely totally on Him, not on your own good works. Will you do this right now?

IF YOU HAVE TRUSTED JESUS CHRIST AS YOUR SAVIOR, THEN YOU CAN KNOW YOU HAVE ETERNAL LIFE. GOD HAS PROMISED THIS IN HIS WORD.

"These things have I written unto you that believe on the name of the Son of God; that ye may <u>know</u> that ye have eternal life, and that ye may believe on the name of the Son of God" (1 John 5:13).

STUDY SECTION

Chapter 1 - The Advent

KEY VERSES:
- Matthew 24:37-39
- 1 Thessalonians 1:10
- Titus 2:13
- 1 Thessalonians 2:19
- Zechariah 12:2-3
- Jeremiah 31:35-36
- 2 Timothy 4:8

HIS ATTRIBUTES

1. List the positive character traits of the Antichrist figure and then ask these questions:
   a. What impact will each character trait have upon the world?
   b. What traits are people looking for in a world leader today?
   c. How will his character traits affect world religions?

2. List the physical attributes of the Antichrist figure and then ask these questions:
   a. How will the world respond to this man?
   b. How will it affect his worldwide appeal?
   c. How will his physical attributes help pave the way for world peace?

3. The era of the Son of Satan will feature a worldwide identification symbol - described ominously in Scripture as "The Mark of the Beast."
   a. Given today's rapid technological advancement, how easy will it be for people to accept this mark?
   b. What arguments will he make to calm people's fears?
   c. What common sense solutions will this mark bring

to centuries-old problems like organized crime and
corruption?
   d. What practical solutions will this mean for everyday
   transactions?
   e. What are some ways in which society is being
   conditioned to accept the Mark of the Beast?

4. Not just "against Christ", he is a "type" of the ultimate
christ, the kind of christ people have always wanted.
   a. Explain the difference between a mere "anti" Christ
   and a "type"of Christ.
   b. Discuss the ways in which the Son of Satan will
   imitate Christ's life on earth.

5. "For all his apparent kindness in his heart, he is a
deceiver, just as his father the devil is a fraud." Why will
people be so easily lured into following the Antichrist?

TODAY'S WORLD
1. Read Matthew 24:37-39 and 2 Peter 3:4.
   a. Compare and contrast the days of Noah with the
   current world situation.
   b. Who are the "scoffers" today and what are their
     arguments?
     1. In the news media
     2. Among skeptical Christians

2. Read Zechariah 12:2-3; Jeremiah 30:10-11; and Jeremiah
31:35-36.
   a. How do recent events fit into Scripture's portrayal of
   the end-times?
   b. How does constant turmoil in the Holy Land fit into
   the prophets' predictions?

WHAT IT MEANS FOR ME
1. What does Bible teacher, Charles U. Wagner mean
when he says, "When Scripture tells him (the believer)

to 'look for that blessed hope' he can do so with a confidence that allows this hope to impact his life spiritually"?

    a. Discuss the ways in which a knowledge of Bible prophecy can give Christians "Spiritual Readiness."

      1. Evangelistic Fervor

      2. Materialistic Outlook

      3. Reshaping of Priorities

    b. Read 1 Thessalonians 2:19; James 5:7; and Titus 2:13.

      1. Make a list of ominous headlines from the last seven days.

      2. Make a list of worries and concerns in your personal life.

      3. Discuss how Scripture's hope gives us peace.

2. Briefly recount the facts regarding Bible prophecy in Chapter 1.

    a. What does Scripture's own emphasis on prophecy tell us about its importance?

    b. Discuss the possible negative effect on a believer who doesn't have at least a working knowledge of Bible prophecy.

    c. Discuss the possible positive effect on a believer who reads and understands Bible prophecy.

3. Read 2 Timothy 4:8 and then find a quiet moment in your day to ask the Lord to help you cultivate an eternal perspective.

    a. Are you motivated by materialism or power or by the eternal needs of lost souls?

    b. Are there areas in your personal life that need growth?

    c. Are you fully committed to your local church?

    d. Are you faithful to your spouse and your family?

    e. Who do you allow to influence your decision making?

Chapter 2 - The Sign

Key Verses:
- Isaiah 14:12-15
- 1 Corinthians 1:7
- 1 Thessalonians 5:23
- 2 Peter 3:4
- 1 John 2:28
- Matthew 24:33
- Matthew 24:4-5
- Matthew 24:23-26

His Attributes

1. When did Satan's campaign against God begin?

2. List the five I's that reveal the depth of Satan's prideful heart.

3. The battle is real. It is still being fought. Right now. All around us. How does this explain the wickedness of our age?
   a. How has Satan blinded the minds of unbelievers?
   b. Who is the real enemy? (Read Ephesians 6:12.)

Today's World

1. Read 1 Corinthians 1:7 and 1 Thessalonians 5:23
   a. Does the Lord rebuke Christians for looking for His Coming?
   b. Christians have been looking to the Rapture since the early church. Does this mean the Rapture is a long way off? Does this mean we're foolish to anticipate His Coming?

2. While there are many signs for what is known as the Second Coming of Christ, there are no signs for the Rapture.
   a. Explain the difference between the Rapture and

the Second Coming.
  b. How can even the most prepared believer be
     surprised at the time of the Rapture?

3. Read Matthew 24:4,5,23,24, and 26.
  a. Does Jesus' prediction of false teachers fit today's
     current state of the Church?
  b. List some of the current movements within the
     Church that point to the soon coming of Christ.
  c. How do we know if a teacher is teaching the right
     things?

4. When we look at the present spiritual and social
   climate, who does it appear has won?
  a. On social issues like abortion, euthanasia, crime,
     and traditional marriage
  b. In pop culture
  c. In international conflicts, especially terrorism and
     anti-Western values
  d. In modern Christianity, with the trend toward
     liberalism and compromise?

5. How does today's dismissive hostility toward
   Christianity resemble the attitude of the citizens of
   Galveston in 1900?

6. What signs in our world let us know that we are
   living in the "season" of the Rapture?

7. How should the imminence of the Rapture affect the
   attitude of a believer?
  a. How does it affect his worldview?
  b. How does it change his outlook?

8. List some possible tragic scenarios that will take place at
   the moment of the Rapture.
  a. How will these help usher in the reign of the

Antichrist?
b. How will this erase national sovereignty?
c. What will this do to people's personal freedoms?

9. We look for the coming of the Lord because there are certain sign that just didn't exist years ago.
   a. List some of the current signs of the times in religion
   b. In politics and government
   c. In international news

WHAT IT MEANS FOR ME
1. Go back to the five I's of Satan's character.
   a. What are five areas in which believers set themselves up as their own gods?
   b. Think of times in your own life where you intentionally or unintentionally set yourself or your will higher than God.
   c. What is the logical conclusion to our rebellion against God?

2. Do you know the Lord as your personal Savior?   If not, flip to the Appendix (before the Study Section.)

   If you have further questions, you can call 1-800-78-GRACE (1-800-784-7223) or check out our special section online at www.victoryingrace.org.

3. Why do Christians have nothing to fear from the Son of Satan?

4. As a true violinist will recognize a true Stradivarius, so a discerning believer will understand and know if what he is being taught is true to the Word of God. Consider your own Bible study.
   a. Are you reading books and literature that affirms the orthodox principles of Scripture?

   b. Have you ever heard Christians that say "doctrine is not important"?

   c. Does your church's statement of faith line up with Scripture?

5. Ryan avoided falling into the trap of false teaching because he was grounded in the Word of God. Consider yourself for a moment.

   a. Are you committed to faithfully attending a Bible-believing and teaching local church?

   b. Do you surround yourself with like-minded believers who affirm your church's teachings?

   c. Do you read and study books that add to your knowledge of Scripture?

   d. Are there any Bible study classes at your church or college- level courses that may enhance your knowledge of Scripture?

Chapter 3 - The Names

KEY VERSES:
- Genesis 3
- Hebrews 2:18
- John 2:22
- Daniel 7:25
- 2 Thessalonians 2:11
- Daniel 11:36
- Revelation 17-18
- 1 John 2:18
- 1 John 4:3-4

HIS ATTRIBUTES

1. What was Satan's motivation in beguiling Adam and Eve?

2. What was it about Adam and Eve's special relationship with God that angered Satan?

3. In spite of her perfect environment, Eve succumbed to Satan's temptation.
    a. What was the one thing Eve didn't have that Satan tempted her with?
    b. What lies did Satan weave that drew in Eve?

4. Why wasn't Eve startled by a talking animal?

5. Compare and contrast Satan's temptation in the Garden and His temptation of the world during the Tribulation.

6. How did Satan's seemingly ingenious plan in the Garden play into the hands of God?

7. How will his plan during the Tribulation period play into the hands of God?

8. List the names of the Son of Satan
   a. How will each evil characteristic affect his rule of the world?
   b. How will he disguise each evil characteristic to fool the masses?

9. Chart the differences in the real Christ and his superficial counterpart, the Antichrist.

10. Why does Satan seek to imitate Christ?

TODAY'S WORLD
1. How are today's social, political, economic and religious trends conditioning people to accept the agenda of the Antichrist?

2. How do the basic tenets of New Age philosophy mirror the philosophy of the Antichrist?

3. Explain how the Holy Spirit's control limits the spread of sin in the world.

4. What effect will the people's trust in this Antichrist have on them?

5. The tragedies of 9/11/01 and other sudden worldwide tragedies have conditioned the world to look to one global leader. How will the Rapture's aftermath pave the way for the Son of Satan's rise in stature?

WHAT IT MEANS FOR ME
1. "If Adam and Eve could have only known the chasm they were nearing, they would never have given the time of day to the Serpent. If they could have fathomed in the smallest degree what their disobedience would do to not only them but to their children and children's children, they probably would have run as fast as they could from

the snake."
   a. What are some ways in which we are deceived into believing Satan's lies?
   b. How does Satan carefully package traps to look innocent?
   c. How often do we stop and consider the repercussions of bowing to sin?
   d. How does Satan distract us from thinking through our decisions?

2. Take a moment right now and ask God to show you where a Mr. or Mrs. Sin may be residing in your life.

3. Adam and Eve had dominion over the Serpent. They could have ordered it to flee the garden. Instead, they willingly became its slave.
   a. As Christians what power do we personally have over sin?
   b. What power do we have at our disposal as the means of overcoming sin?
   c. What mistake do we often make when confronted with temptation?

4. Read Hebrews 2:18. What relief does Jesus' temptation bring to our own situations?

5. Having seen the true motivations of Satan, the prince and power of the air, how should that color our view of the world?

Chapter 4 - The Conceit

KEY VERSES:
- Job 1-2
- 1 Chronicles 21
- 2 Chronicles 12:7
- 1 John 1:9
- Job 42:12-17
- 2 Thessalonians 2:4
- Revelation 13:11-14

HIS ATTRIBUTES

1. What is behind Satan's plan to bring forth the Man of Sin to deceive the world?

2. Why does Satan seek to bring down dedicated followers of Christ?

3. Name some of the great leaders in Scripture whom Satan has tempted.

4. In what way does Satan seek to destroy churches?

5. How does 2 Thessalonians 2:4 explain the depths of the Antichrist's pride?

6. Read Revelation 13:11-14.
   - a. What skill will enable the False Prophet to direct all acclaim and adoration toward the Antichrist?
   - b. Briefly discuss the characteristics of the False Prophet
   - c. How will he disguise his evil intentions?
   - d. How will he incorporate the spiritual dimension of the Antichrist's agenda?

7. Read Revelation 13:11-14 and Daniel 3. How does the worship of the Antichrist resemble the worshipping

of the image during the reign of Nebuchadnezzar?

TODAY'S WORLD

1. Why is Satan not completely successful in his race to conquer the human race and turn them all away from God?

2. Why will the world be ripe for total evil at the Rapture?

3. How does Satan's plan only further God's ultimate plan for the world?

4. Explain how prophecy illustrates mercy on the part of God instead of cruelty.

5. The Antichrist will declare himself to be God and demand total allegiance.
    a. How will the world accept this?
    b. What will he do to condition their response?
    c. How is the world being conditioned today?

6. How will the signs and wonders of the False Prophet deceive the world?

7. What are some disturbing trends in the church that are conditioning the masses to accept these signs and wonders?

8. The False Prophet will build a graven image and demand its worship.
    a. In whose spirit will the image be created?
    b. Discuss the hype surrounding this ceremony
    c. What will this do to "freedom of worship"?
    d. How is today's current religious and social climate being prepared for the worship of one false god?

WHAT IT MEANS FOR ME

1. Reread the dramatized account of Satan's attack on Job. Answer these questions:

   a. Why do you think Satan desired to bring down Job?

   b. What characteristics did Job possess in His life that:

     i. Made Satan angry and jealous?

     ii. Led God to say, "There is no greater servant."

2. " . . . the humans created seemed to love God on their own."

   a. What is it about the Christian faith that separates it from world religions?

   b. Why is it that Christians in impoverished countries often have a deeper faith than those in more developed countries?

   c. What is it about trials that increases our faith?

   d. What is the greatest danger to a Christian persecution or materialism?

3. The closer you draw to Jesus, the more direct will be the attack of the enemy. What steps must we take to combat the enemy?

4. Given Satan's desire to bring down churches, what does that tell us about our attitude toward our church?

5. How should Job's refusal to curse God inspire us?

6. What lesson does Job's testimony have for us when we are persecuted?

   a. When we're tempted to complain and murmur against God and his people.

   b. When we're tempted to blame others for our problems.

7. What promise do we have from the Lord that protects us from Satan's attacks?

8. Satan didn't want to think that people could simply love God for who He is and not for what He has given them.
   a. How do we react when we've lost everything?
   b. Do any of these motivate us for service?
      i. Prestige among our Christians peers
      ii. Material blessings and prosperity
      iii. Pride
   c. What should be the real motivation for service?

9. How can and should the agenda of the False Prophet get us excited about God's plan for the ages?
   a. What does it tell us about the authenticity of Scripture?
   b. What does it reveal about the character of God?
   c. What does it say about the lure of worldliness?

Chapter 5 - The Humanist

KEY VERSES:
- 1 Samuel 17
- 1 Chronicles 21
- Daniel 11:37
- Daniel 2:31-35
- Matthew 24:15
- Philippians 2:10-11

HIS ATTRIBUTES:

1. What ideology did Satan use to bring down David?

2. What is the central tenet of humanism?

3. Why is humanism so opposed to Christianity?

4. Read Daniel 11:37. Explain how the Antichrist will more than just reject the one true God.

5. Why does Satan attack believers after a spiritual victory?

TODAY'S WORLD

1. How does today's current New Age philosophy line up with the teachings of the Antichrist?

2. How will humanism pave the way for the eventual rule of the Son of Satan?

3. How did the discovery of the Dead Sea scrolls validate the historical accuracy of the book of Daniel?

4. Read Daniel 2:31-35. How does this describe the empires of the world?

5. Read Philippians 2:10-11. What does this say about the

future of Satan's plan?

6. What does it say about the future of humanism, atheism, and liberalism?

WHAT IT MEANS FOR ME

1. Explain how focusing on the gift rather than the Giver often leads us into temptation.

2. Why does Satan grow angry when Christians trust God?

3. How does Satan tempt those who trust God the most?

4. Why do Christians struggle to overcome humanism?

5. What is the danger of secular humanism?

6. What does humanism encourage believers to do?

7. Why do those who sin against what they know pay more dearly than those who do not know?

8. What lesson did David's sin have for the children of Israel?

9. What lesson does it have for Christians today?

10. Go back to Chapter 5 and reread the prayer at the end of the chapter.

Chapter 6 - The Unholy Trinity

KEY VERSES:
- Matthew 4:1-11
- Hebrews 4:15
- Revelation 11:13-14
- John 8:44
- Revelation 13:11
- John 16:14
- Revelation 16:13; 19:20; 20:10
- 2 Corinthians 11:14,15
- Revelation 12:11
- Revelation 1:5

HIS ATTRIBUTES

1. Reread the temptations of Satan in the first five chapters. What is his primary pattern?

    a. When does he usually strike the believer?

    b. What message does he usually bring?

2. What was the difference between Satan's temptations of sinful men and his temptations of Jesus?

3. What three entities will comprise the unholy Trinity?

4. Why does Satan attempt to counterfeit God?

5. Where do the prophecies of the False Prophet originate?

6. Explain the unholy Trinity's attempt to hijack Christianity and make it palatable to the masses.

TODAY'S WORLD

1. Why is Islamic fundamentalism too exclusive for Satan's agenda?

2. How have events like September 11 and the fall of
   Hussein's regime in Iraq exposed the roots of Islamic
   fundamentalism?

3. Explain how democracy, while a positive government
   system, actually helps to usher in the agenda of the
   Antichrist.

4. What does author Dave Hunt mean when he says,
   "The collapse of communism in Eastern Europe and the
   introduction of 'freedom of religion' is not a setback for
   Satan"?

5. Why is the new world order proposed by the first
   President Bush a bad thing?

WHAT IT MEANS FOR ME

1. Think back to your times of greatest temptation. Were
   they usually preceded by a spiritual victory?

2. What warning should this give to Christians?

3. The last chapter has been written, and Satan's
   attempts at victory only bring God's timetable for the
   end-times closer.
     a. How does this truth help us in our conflicts?
        i. At work
        ii. At home
     b. What hope does this give us about the rapid
        erosion of our values in America?
     c. What hope does this give us about the slow
        encroachment upon our religious freedoms?

4. Find the prayer at the end of Chapter 6. Pray this prayer
   today.

Chapter 7 - The False Sacrifice

KEY VERSES:
- Matthew 8:28-32
- Mark 13:14-20
- John 20:29

HIS ATTRIBUTES:
1. What is the significance of Satan's sacrifice of a pig in the Holy of Holies?

2. For what miracle of Jesus is this act a retaliation?

3. Read Mark 13:14-20
    a. What warning does Satan's abomination give to the Jewish people?
    b. What does this warning prove about God's mercy?
    c. What does Satan's sacrifice prove about his character?

TODAY'S WORLD
1. Those who criticize a literal interpretation of the Bible with regard to end times say that it teaches Christians to sit on their hands and wait for the Rapture.
    a. How do the signs God gives disprove that theory?
    b. How does the presence of the 144K evangelists disprove that theory.
    c. How does God's mercy disprove that theory?

2. How does today's rash of incurable diseases fit into the end-times scenario?

3. What does the existence of end-times prophecy show us about skeptics who demand "to see it before they will believe it"?

4. What does Israel's desire to rebuild the temple prove

about the closeness of Jesus' coming? What prophecies will this help fulfill?

5. Visit templeinstitute.org and look up the various instruments needed to rebuild the temple. Jot down a few notes about each one:
   a. Their significance
   b. Updates on their status
   c. What Jewish people are saying about them

What It Means For Me

1. God, in His Word, has given signs to show the impending judgment of the world. What lessons does this have for us as Christians?
   a. What signs is God showing you and me about our personal lives?
   b. What mercy has God exhibited toward us in the midst of His judgment in our lives?

2. What is the purpose of pain in our lives?

3. Why doesn't God unload all of His judgment at once?

4. What should our response be to prophecy:
   a. Sit on our hands and wait for the Rapture?
   b. Engage ourselves in God's work to save others from tasting His future judgment?

5. Even though we see prophecy fulfilled almost daily, why must we still walk by faith?

6. Why will there be no excuse for those who reject Christ?

Chapter 8 - The Prosperity

KEY VERSES:
- John 13:18-27
- John 12:5-6
- Genesis 2:10-11, 13-15
- Genesis 10:8-10
- Genesis 11
- Daniel 2:31-35
- Daniel 11:21
- Revelation 14:7-8
- Jeremiah 50:1-3
- Jeremiah 51:47-48
- Revelation 18:2-12
- Isaiah 13:19-22
- Jeremiah 51:24-26
- Mathew 24:2
- Revelation 17-18

HIS ATTRIBUTES
1. Who was the real mastermind behind Judas' betrayal of Jesus?

2. What was Satan's motivation in betraying Jesus?

3. What has our study shown us about Satan's desire to destroy?

4. What has happened to every evil plan of Satan?

5. Why is Babylon so crucial to the agenda of the Son of Satan?

6. Why is it crucial for God's plan for the ages?

TODAY'S WORLD
1. List the different theories as to the future of Babylon.

2. What are some current facts that point to the U.S. as Babylon?

3. Why is it significant that the U.S. and Babylon are currently linked through our involvement in Iraq?

4. Read Genesis 10:8-10. What does this passage tell us about the roots of Babylon?

5. Read Genesis 11. What does this passage tell us about Babylon's religion and its worldwide influence?

6. What end-times ideology is typified in the Tower of Babel?

7. What four empires are represented in Nebuchadnezzar's dream in Daniel 2:31-35?

8. What is represented by "the great stone cut without hands"?

9. What does the U.S.'s failure to fall possibly tell us about its future in end-times prophecy?

10. What do recent developments tell us about America's position in the world?
    a. Is it weakening or declining?
    b. What does the United States' role in Iraq possibly signify?
    c. Is Europe poised to take over?

11. What does Revelation tell us about the world's future economic situation?
    a. Will it get better or worse?
    b. If the Rapture were to occur now, what country would be most affected?

   c. Could this be the country about whose fall "the world weeps"?

12. What affect does peace and prosperity have on society?
   a. Does it make people more sensitive to spiritual matters?
   b. Does it heighten their awareness of danger?

13. What does the historical record tell us about Babylon's destruction?

WHAT IT MEANS FOR ME

1. What weakness in Judas did Satan exploit?

2. How can we guard ourselves against his temptations?

3. What hope do Satan's defeats give us in our daily struggles?

Chapter 9 - The Seal

KEY VERSES:
- Acts 5:1-11
- Revelation 7
- Matthew 24:45
- Revelation 7:9
- Revelation 20:4
- Revelation 7:15
- 2 Corinthians 4:17-18

HIS ATTRIBUTES

1. Read Acts 5:1-11.
   a. What was the real sin of Ananias and Sapphira?
   b. How did they become a tool of the Devil?

2. What is the job of the 144, 000 Jewish evangelists?

3. How will they be distinguished from the followers of the Son of Satan?

4. Why will there be no second chance for those who take the Mark of the Beast?

5. What will the Son of Satan do to those who accept Jesus?

6. Read Revelation 7:9. How are the martyrs distinct from the 144K?

TODAY'S WORLD

1. Even though the consequences are greater, in what way will sharing the gospel be easier during the Tribulation?

2. In contrast to today's prosperity, how will the events of the Tribulation affect how people look at spirituality?

3. What will be the future of those who will be martyred for their faith?

4. List some of the religious groups who have claimed the mantle of the 144K.

5. What evidence in Scripture tells us that none of these groups is indeed the 144, 000?

6. Read Revelation 7:9. What does this tell us about the number of souls saved during the ministry of the 144K?

WHAT IT MEANS FOR ME

1. What lesson does the punishment of Ananias and Saphira have for us?

2. Read and meditate on Revelation 7. You may want to post it on your refrigerator.
   a. How should this passage inspire us to Christian service?
   b. What does it tell us about the depths of God's love and mercy for a fallen and sinful world?

3. The 144K will carry a seal of the Holy Spirit upon their forehead. What seal do Christians have?
   a. How do we often undermine our mission by our forays into worldliness?
   b. What does this tell us about our testimony before unsaved people?

4. Go back to Chapter 9 and think about the promises of God.

5. Read 2 Corinthians 4:17-18. How can this encourage us in times of trial?

Chapter 10 - The Witnesses

KEY VERSES:
- Matthew 18:16
- Revelation 11:1-19
- 2 Kings 1:10
- Revelation 11:5
- 1 Kings 1:13-14
- 1 Kings 17:1
- 2 Kings 2:11-12
- Hebrews 9:27
- Revelation 11:5-6
- Genesis 5:22-24
- Zechariah 4:1-6
- Matthew 10:28

THEIR ATTRIBUTES

1. What was the value of witnesses in Jewish Law?

2. List some of the courageous deeds of the two witnesses.

3. Read Revelation 11:5-6. Who does this seem to describe?

4. List some of the facts that lead us to believe Elijah is one of the witnesses.

5. List some of the facts that lead Bible scholars to believe Moses is one of the witnesses.

6. List some of the facts that lead Bible scholars to believe Enoch is one of the witnesses.

7. What was unique about Enoch's life?

8. What was special about his era?

9. Explain how the death of the witnesses will be claimed as a triumph of Satan.

10. Explain how it merely fits into God's prophetic plan.

11. What stops Satan from controlling the witnesses?

TODAY'S WORLD
1. What does the ministry of the two witnesses reveal about the character of God?

2. How have recent events in the news and pop culture desensitized people to witnessing death and destruction on television?

3. How will people respond to the decaying bodies of the two witnesses?

4. What will this massive earthquake do to Jerusalem?

5. Read Revelation 11:4 and Zechariah 4:1-6. What do these passages reveal about the two witnesses?

6. What about the witnesses tells us God is dealing with the Jewish people during the Tribulation?

WHAT IT MEANS FOR ME
1. What effect should a knowledge of God's mercy throughout the ages have on Christians?
   a. How should we view trials and circumstances?
   b. How should we treat others who wrong us?

2. Repeat the prayer given at the end of chapter 10. Meditate on God's mercy.

Chapter 11 - The Battle

KEY VERSES:
- Revelation 16
- Revelation 19:11-20:6
- Revelation 6
- Revelation 8:7-9
- Joel 2:30-31
- Revelation 9
- Revelation 12:6

HIS ATTRIBUTES

1. Where will the battle of Armageddon be fought?

2. What topography makes this site a logical place for a world war?

3. How will this battle differ from the Armageddon portrayed in popular culture?

4. How will believers fight with the Lord against the Devil?

5. What do each of the four horsemen represent?

6. Who are the people contained in the fifth seal?

7. What is contained in the sixth seal?

8. List the trumpet judgments and what they represent.

9. List the bowl judgments and what they represent.

10. What effect does each judgment have on Satan's grip on the world?

TODAY'S WORLD

1. How does the severity of the judgments refute the theory of a mid- Tribulation rapture?

2. Explain why these judgments are just "the beginning of sorrows."

3. Read Revelation 9:6. Explain the horror and torture of this judgment.

4. Why does Petra make an excellent hiding place for the Jewish people?

5. How does God protect His remnant throughout the worst of judgment?

6. How does God protect the church, His Bride, during today's cultural decline?

WHAT IT MEANS FOR ME

1. What small comfort can the martyrs take?

2. Why is it important for Christians to stand fast in this dark age?

Chapter 12 - The Last Battle

KEY VERSES:
- Revelation 20:4-6
- Daniel 2:31-35
- Zechariah 14:8-21
- Isaiah 2:2-4
- Isaiah 11:6
- Isaiah 65:17-25
- Revelation 10:7-10
- Revelation 20:11-15
- Ecclesiastes 12:14
- Revelation 21:2-8

HIS ATTRIBUTES

1. What argument does the scenario in Revelation 20 do away with?

2. How can Satan's absence still bring about wickedness?

3. What is the clear message given to the prophets about Israel's bleak condition?

4. How can there be so many people who reject God after a time of perfect peace and order in the Millennium?

5. Describe the utopian environment of the 1,000 year reign of Christ.

6. Explain this thought: "Even in the absence of worldly temptations and the devil, man is still capable of rebellion against God."

7. How does this square with humanism?

8. How does the reality of the Great White Throne Judgment do away with the theory that Hell is

annihilation?

9. What happens to Satan at the end of the millennium?

10. What was Satan's real role in the grand scheme of God's master plan?

Today's World
1. What are the two "distant peaks" of the Lord's coming?

2. Explain the difference between the Rapture and the Second Coming.

3. Explain the difference between the two resurrections.

4. Write down the six reasons for belief in a premillenial view of the Lord's return.

5. Read Zechariah 14:8-21. Explain the importance of Jerusalem during the Tribulation and Millennium.

6. What hope should God's future plan for Israel give to Jewish people today?

7. What will believers do during the Millennium?

8. What does the reality of the Millennium do for our view of the environment?

9. Who is judged at the Great White Throne?

10. What is meant by "degrees of Hell?"

11. By what authority will these people be judged?

What It Means for Me

1. If Satan were taken out of the picture and all temptations were removed, would that make it easier not to sin? Would you and I be automatically perfect?

2. What does the depravity of man's heart evidenced at the end of the Millennium tell us about our own hearts?

3. What does it tell us about our frequent excuses for sin?

4. What is God's method for change in believers?

5. Meditate this week on your heart. Ask yourself these questions:
    a. How tempted am I to follow my heart?
    b. What is my true motivation for life?
    c. Am I allowing God to change me from the inside?

6. What are three benefits of believers during the Millennium?

7. How should the reality of the Great White Throne Judgment affect our motivation as believers?
    a. Our witnessing
    b. Our testimony
    c. Our walk with God

8. What is the promise God leaves us with at the end of Revelation?

9. Meditate this week on the last two chapters of the book of Revelation. Flip back to these anytime you grow discouraged or weary in the work of Christ.

NOTES

CHAPTER 1
THE ADVENT

1. Richard C. Paddock and Al Jacinto, "Hostages Killed as Philippine Troops Track Down Kidnappers," *Los Angeles Times,* June 8, 2002.
2. James R Adair, *The Man and His Ministry*, (Grand Rapids, MI: Zondervan Publishing House, 1969) p. 157.
3. "Church Gates Become Must-Have for Thieves," *This is Local London,* May 17, 2000, Newsquest Media Group, A Gannet Company.
4. Dave Hunt, *How Close Are We?*, (Eugene, OR: Harvest House Publishers, 1993) p. 313.
5. Charles Ryrie, et al, *Countdown to Armageddon*, (Eugene, OR: Harvest House Publishers, 1999) p 37.
6. John Stensrud, "Are We Really Living in the Last Times?" , Sermoncentral.com, June 20, 2002.
7. I.J. Toby Westerman, "Female Terrorist Does An About Face," *World Net Daily,* June 21, 2002.
8. "Saddam Hussein Praises Palestinian Suicide Attacks, " Al Bawaba, INA news agency, Arutz-7, June 21, 2002.
9. Dave Hunt, p. 33.
10. Reuters, November 3, 2003,
11. Charles Ryrie, et al, p. 13.
12. As quoted in Evie Megginson, "Second Coming," Sermoncentral.com, June 21, 2002.
13. *Our Daily Bread*, January 12, 1995.

CHAPTER 2
THE SIGN

1. Tim LaHaye and Jerry B. Jenkins, *Are We Living In The End Times?*, (Wheaton, IL, Tyndale House Publishers, 1999) p.21.
2. Dave Hunt, *How Close Are We?*, (Eugene, OR: Harvest House Publishers) p. 116
3. Thomas Ice, "Why God's Purpose for the Tribulation Excludes the Church," The Thomas Ice Collection, Raptureready.com.
4. John Walvoord, *Prophecy Knowledge Handbook*, (Wheaton IL, Victor Books, 1990) p. 251.
5. *Antiques Road Show Calendar,* (New York, NY, Workman Publishers, 2001). p. 251.

Chapter 3
The Names

1. Erwin Lutzer, *The Serpent of Paradise* (Chicago, IL, Moody Press, 1996), pp.49-50.
2. Mark Cambron, *Son of Satan* (Chicago, IL, Moody Press, 1945), p. 21
3. Ibid. p. 22.

Chapter 4
The Conceit

1. Chris Armstrong, "Preacher in the Hand of an Angry Church," Leadership Journal, Winter 2003, pp. 52-53.
2. "Jordan's King of Disguise," BBC News, July 30, ww.news.bbc.co.uk/1/hi/world/middle_east.
3. Tim LaHaye, *The Merciful God of Prophecy,* (New York, Warner Books, 2002), p. 12).

Chapter 5
The Humanist

1. John F. Walvoord, *The Prophecy Knowledge Handbook*, (Wheaton, IL Victor Books, 1990) p. 212-213.
2. Ray C. Stedman, *What's This World Coming To?* (Ventura, CA: Regal Books, 1970) p. 43
3. Walvoord, p. 272.

Chapter 6
The Unholy Trinity

1. Edgar C James, *Armageddon and the New World Order*, (Chicago, IL, Moody Press, 1991) pp. 51-52.
2. M.R.De Haan, *The Revelation Record*, (Wheaton, IL Tyndale House Publishers, 1983) p.246.
3. Dave Hunt, *Global Peace and the Rise of the Antichrist*, (Eugene, OR: Harvest House Publishers, 1990) p. 249.
4. Ibid., pp. 160-161.
5. Sam F. Ghattas, "Iraqi Information Minister Uses Insults," The Associated Press, Tuesday, April 8, 2003; 2:26 PM.
6. Erwin Lutzer, *The Serpent of Paradise*, (Chicago, IL, Moody Press, 1996) p. 176.

CHAPTER 7
THE FALSE SACRIFICE

1. Tim LaHaye, *The Merciful God of Prophecy,* (New York, Warner Books, 2002), p. 82.
2. Michael D. Lemonic, Alice Park, Michele, Orecklin, "The Truth About SARS, The Surprising Impact of SARS," Time, May 5, 2003, p20
3. John Wesley White, *The Coming World Dictator,* Minneapolis, Bethany Fellowship, 1981, p. 90).
4. Pinchas H. Pell, "*The Significance of Sacrifice,"* Jerusalem Post International Edition, Week ending March 30, 1985, p. 10.
5. Pinchas H. Pell, "A Place for the Lord," Jerusalem Post, February 11, 1989.
6. "Time for a New Temple?" Time, October 16, 1989.
7. Mortimer Zuckerman, *US News and World Report*, November 12, 1990, pp. 95-96.
8. "The Mississippi-Red Heifer Update," *The Restoration,* May/June 1995,PO Box 31714, Jerusalem, Israel. US contact, Mr. L. Goldsmith, 1438 East 34th Street, Brooklyn, NY 11234. Phone/Fax: (718) 338-3158.

CHAPTER 8
THE PROSPERITY

1 Mark Hitchcock, *The Second Coming of Babylon*, (Sisters, OR: Multnomah Publishers, Inc. 2003) p.39.
2. Charles H. Dyer, *The Rise of Babylon* (Chicago, IL, Moody Publishers, 1991, revised 2003) p. 98.
3. As quoted in Bernard Lewis, *The Arabs in History*, rev. ed. (New York, Evanston, San Francisco, London: Harper-Colophon Books, 1966), pp. 31-32.

CHAPTER 9
THE SEAL

1. John Ankerberg and John Weldon, *Encyclopedia of Cults and New Religions,* (Eugene, OR: Harvest House Publishers, 1999) p. 186.

CHAPTER 10
THE WITNESSES

1. Tim LaHaye and Jerry Jenkins, *Tribulation Force*, (Wheaton, IL: Tyndale House Publishers), p. 295
2. Ray Stedman, "The Last Warning" Series: Revelation , Message No: 15,

Catalog No: 4203, February 25, 1990, sermoncentral.com.
3. ibid, Ray Stedman.
4. John Walvoord, *Prophecy Knowledge Handbook,* (Wheaton, IL: Victor Books, 1990), p. 575.

CHAPTER 11
THE BATTLE

1. Tim LaHaye, *Revelation Illustrated and Made Plain*, (Grand Rapids, MI: Zondervan Publishing House, 1975), p. 98
2. Ibid, p. 219.

CHAPTER 12
THE LAST BATTLE

1. Brenda Rotzoll "Students' Web Project Remembers Victims of Bataan Death March," Warner, *Chicago Sun Times*, Monday August 18, 2003.
2. Clarence Larkin, *Dispensational Truth*, pp. 300.